The Smart Home Buyer

By

Marc Saint Clair, MBA

The Smart Home Buyer

Disclaimer

The information presented in this book is based on the author's extensive experience as a broker spanning over 15 years. While every effort has been made to ensure the accuracy and relevance of the content, real estate markets can vary significantly over time and across regions. Therefore, the author and publisher cannot guarantee the current applicability or accuracy of the information contained herein.

This book is intended for general informational purposes only and should not be construed as professional advice. Readers are encouraged to consult with qualified professionals, such as financial advisors, real estate attorneys, or mortgage lenders, before making any financial or real estate decisions.

The mention of specific market trends, strategies, or practices reflects the author's perspective at the time of writing and may not necessarily apply to all situations or future market conditions. The author and publisher disclaim any liability for any damages or losses incurred directly or indirectly from the use or application of the information presented in this book.

All rights reserved. No part of this publication may be reproduced, distributed, or transmitted in any form or by any means, including photocopying, recording, or other electronic or mechanical methods, without the prior written permission of the publisher, except in the case of brief quotations embodied in critical reviews and certain other noncommercial uses permitted by copyright law.

Marc Saint Clair, MBA

Acknowledgment

My name is Marc Saint Clair, and I have been in the real estate business since 2007 in the state of Massachusetts. I became a broker in 2009, and I hold a master's degree in business administration (MBA) with a focus on entrepreneurship. Over the years, I have helped many first-time home buyers, minorities, and novice investors navigate the complex process of buying a home. I am known for using unconventional approaches to help my clients get their offers accepted, even in the harshest market conditions.

This book aims to help potential buyers make better-educated decisions when buying a home. I want to open their eyes to the many factors they should consider before making a purchase. Through this book, I will guide readers through the basics of understanding a particular market and provide tips and advice on navigating the buying process, from selecting an agent, home inspections, and financing to smart home buying tips in every chapter.

The intended audience for this book is first-time home buyers and/or individuals seeking to change their living space. The housing market is full of pitfalls, and it is crucial for buyers to understand the risks involved and how to assess them. By providing clear and concise information, I hope to help these individuals make informed decisions and find the perfect home for their needs.

I would like to add, first and foremost, my heartfelt thanks to God because I can do nothing on this earth without His grace. I acknowledge my wife, Veronique Saint Clair, for pushing me to write this book. She always tells me that I am a walking encyclopedia for home buyers and sellers and that I should share my knowledge with others. It took more than five years of encouragement, but I finally decided to finish this book this year. She is my rock, my foundation, and my number-one fan.

I want to extend special thanks to Eunice Depina at Harborone Bank, who answered many of my questions and provided invaluable

The Smart Home Buyer

knowledge and patience. I would also like to thank Randy Wilburn, my first broker, who taught me much and instilled trust in me.

I wrote this book with the goal of providing helpful information to first-time home buyers and homeowners seeking to change their living space. With high interest rates, low inventory, and high prices now, buying a home has become increasingly challenging. However, I believe that purchasing a home can be a significant initial step, and possibly the only measure, for some individuals. That's why I want to ensure they have the knowledge and resources to make informed decisions.

By reading this book, I hope to help readers understand the benefits of owning a property and how to make informed decisions when buying.

Marc Saint Clair, MBA

A Step-by-Step Guide

Step 1 – What You Need Before You Start

    1. Work History & Income
    2. Debt-to-Income Ratio
    3. Co-Borrowers & Co-Signers
    4. Credit Score
    5. Mortgage & Down Payment Requirements

Step 2 – Start The Search

    6. Pre-Approval Letter
    7. Real Estate Representation
    8. Get a Real Estate Attorney

Step 3 – Getting Your Property

    9. The Search
    10. Condos
    11. Offer and Deal Structure

Step 4 – My Offer is Accepted, Now What?

    12. Inspection
    13. Purchase and Sales Agreement

Step 5 – Close

    14. After Purchase and Sales & Before Closing
    15. The Closing

Step 6 – Bonus

    16. Buying without a buyer agent
    17. Home Ownership by Non-US Citizens

The Smart Home Buyer

Table of Contents

Disclaimer ii

Acknowledgment iii

A Step-by-Step Guide v

Step One What You Need Before You Start 1

    Chapter 1 Work History & Income 2

    Chapter 2 Debt-to-Income Ratio (DTI) 4

    Chapter 3 Co-Borrowers & Co-Signers 6

    Chapter 4 Credit Score 8

    Chapter 5 Mortgages & Down Payment Requirements 17

Step Two Start The Search 36

    Chapter 6 Pre-approval letter 37

    Chapter 7 Real Estate Representation 40

    Chapter 8 Real Estate Attorney 47

Step Three Getting Your Property 49

    Chapter 9 The Search 50

    Chapter 10 Condos 57

    Chapter 11 Offer and Deal Structure 62

Step Four My Offer is Accepted, Now What? 70

    Chapter 12 Inspection 71

    Chapter 13 Purchase and Sales Agreement 74

Step Five Close 76

    Chapter 14 After Purchase and Sale & Before Closing 77

    Chapter 15 The Closing 79

Step Six Bonus 85

Marc Saint Clair, MBA

Chapter 16 Buying Without a Buyer Agent: A New Era 86

Chapter 17 Home Owership by Non-Citizens 91

Conclusion 98

Marc Saint Clair, MBA

Step One
What You Need Before You Start

As you begin your search for a house, the first step in the buying process is to prepare to obtain a pre-approval from a lender. Preparation involves positioning yourself to not only get the loan, but also to receive a competitive interest rate from your lender. Here are a few things that will help you to secure a competitive loan package.

Chapter 1
Work History & Income

Getting a mortgage requires demonstrating to your lender that you have a stable and predictable source of income. This is achieved by showing a work history of at least two consecutive years in the same profession. However, some exceptions may apply.

If you have changed jobs but are still working in the same occupation, you may still be eligible as long as you have worked in that occupation for two consecutive years.

If you had to take a leave of absence, you may still be eligible as long as you can prove that the leave was for a reasonable reason, such as receiving chemotherapy or taking care of a newborn. Most lenders will accept less than a two-year work history after an extended leave as long as you have been in your current job for at least six months and can provide documentation to prove that you had a two-year consecutive work history in the same occupation prior to your leave. If you have multiple jobs, the full-time job must be the one with a two-year history.

Recent Graduates

Recent graduates may also be eligible with a work history of less than two years as long as they can provide school documentation of their new degree and are employed in a job related to that degree. Some lenders may require a six-month minimum on the new job before granting a pre-approval. For example, if you have been working at a hospital as a Patient Administration Specialist for over two years and then went to school to become a Social Worker. After graduation, if you took a Social Worker job at that hospital, instead of a two-year history, they would qualify you for a loan at the completion of your 6th month of employment as a new grad.

Self Employed

Some lenders may require a stable three-year work history, depending on the profession. If you earn income from self-employment, investments, retirement, social security, or alimony, some lenders may request a three-year income history.

Unemployment

If you have lost your job and are receiving unemployment benefits at the time of purchase, you may have difficulty getting a pre-approval or closing on the loan.

If your job is seasonal and you receive unemployment income during part of the year, you may still be eligible as long as you have a two-year history of collecting seasonal unemployment. Some lenders may require that you receive actual wages at the time of closing. If this applies to you, it is important to talk to the lenders you plan to use to see if they have more favorable flexibility.

Tips:

- Make sure to have a two-year work history at the time of application. If you are planning on getting a home and changing professions at the same time, it may be best to get the home first before switching careers.
- Overtime, bonuses, and commissions are generally not included in your average income if you have been employed for less than two consecutive years.
- Try to avoid applying for or closing on a loan during a period of unemployment cycle.

Chapter 2
Debt-to-Income Ratio (DTI)

Debt-to-income (DTI) ratio is the percentage of your gross monthly income that goes towards paying your monthly debt payment. DTI ratio is a crucial factor that lenders consider when determining how much mortgage you can afford. It is calculated by dividing your monthly debt payments by your pre-tax monthly income and expressed as a percentage. The higher your DTI ratio, it means that you have a higher level of debt versus income. Conversely, a low debt-to-income ratio means that you have less debt when compared to your income, and that is where you want to be. The general cut-off for most lenders is around 40-43%. If your DTI ratio exceeds this limit, it can be difficult to secure a loan.

For example, even if you earn a high income of 200K+ per year, having multiple credit cards, cars, and other recurring monthly debt obligations can make it challenging to secure a mortgage. The lender will not only look at your income, but also your availability of disposable income.

How to calculate debt to income ratio:

1. Add up all your monthly debt payments.
2. Add up all your monthly gross income.
3. Divide your debts by your monthly gross income.
4. Convert the number into a percentage.

Tips:

- Retire as many short-term debts as possible before applying for a mortgage.
- Putting your student loans in forbearance can help lower your

Marc Saint Clair, MBA

debt-to-income ratio during the loan application process.

- If you are a co-borrower on another loan or debt that does not belong to you, it can impact your underwriting process.

Chapter 3
Co-Borrowers & Co-Signers

If you don't have great credit or if your income is too low to qualify for your desired home, you may add one or more co-borrowers or co-signers to your mortgage application to strengthen it. This can result in a lower interest rate and a higher mortgage limit. The co-borrower and co-signer's income, credit history, and assets will be thoroughly scrutinized by the lender to determine their creditworthiness. Co-borrowers and co-signers have similar functions, and they help strengthen the loan application. They are also responsible for the loan in case of default.

Co-borrower

A co-borrower has equal ownership of the property and is equally responsible for the mortgage payments. If you are married, both parties do not have to be on the mortgage if one spouse alone can carry the mortgage. Even though the other spouse is not on the mortgage, you can ask the lender to include the other spouse on the deed before closing. Depending on the lender and loan type, the co-borrower and co-signer do not have to be an occupant of the property.

Veterans Affairs (VA) loans require that the co-borrower is married or is a domestic partner to the borrower, while the Federal Housing Administration loan (FHA) and some conventional loans allow for non-occupying co-borrowers.

Co-Signer

It is important to note the difference between a co-signer and a co-borrower. A co-signer is a family member or a friend that allows you to use their credit and their income at the time of application. A co-signer is liable for the loan if you default but do not have any ownership of the property. If you fail to make your mortgage payment on time, they will be liable for the loan as well.

The main difference between a co-borrower and a co-signer is that the co-signer has no ownership interest in the property.

Tips:

- Choose your co-borrowers wisely.
- Some lenders use the credit score of the weakest borrower, so ask potential lenders if they use the stronger or weakest credit co-borrower during the lender shopping process.
- Your co-borrower's buying power may decrease after co-borrowing as the mortgage will increase their debt-to-income ratio.

Chapter 4
Credit Score

A credit score provides the lender with an insight into your credit risk and lending worthiness.

There are three credit reporting companies: Trans Union, Experian, and Equifax. Each credit report for the average person may have a different score, with a lower score, a higher score, and a middle score. Most lenders use the middle score for evaluating your credit worthiness, while others rely on one or more of their preferred scores.

Terminologies:

FICO Score:

The FICO Score is a credit scoring model the Fair Isaac Corporation developed. It is the most widely used and recognized credit scoring model in the United States. FICO Scores range from 300 to 850 and are calculated based on data from credit bureaus (Equifax, Experian, and TransUnion). FICO Scores consider payment history, credit utilization, length of credit history, credit mix, and new credit. Each credit bureau may have slightly different versions of the FICO Score, and lenders may use specific versions tailored to their industry, such as auto or mortgage lending.

VantageScore:

VantageScore is another credit scoring model developed by the three major credit bureaus. It was created as an alternative to the FICO Score. VantageScores also range from 300 to 850, and similar to FICO Scores, they consider factors such as payment history, credit utilization, credit age, credit mix, and recent credit behavior. However, VantageScore's specific algorithms and weightings may differ from those of the FICO Score. VantageScore 3.0 and 4.0 are the most commonly used versions.

Marc Saint Clair, MBA

Credit Score:

"Credit score" is a more general term that refers to any numerical representation of an individual's creditworthiness. It can encompass both FICO Scores and VantageScores and other scoring models developed by lenders or credit monitoring services. Various credit scores may have different ranges, algorithms, and factors considered. Some lenders may use their proprietary scoring models or industry-specific scores, which can differ significantly from FICO Scores and Vantage Scores.

It's important to note that FICO Score and VantageScore are the most widely used and respected credit scoring models. However, individual lenders and institutions can use the scoring model of their choice or consider additional factors beyond credit scores when evaluating creditworthiness.

FICO

FICO Score and VantageScore are specific credit scoring models with their methodologies, while "credit score" is a broader term encompassing any numerical representation of creditworthiness. FICO score is more widely used for mortgages

Depending on the lender's backing entity, the minimum credit score needed to buy a home range from 620 to 660. I've seen people close on a home with far lower scores with different programs.

The Fair Isaac Corporation (FICO) introduced its credit scoring model in 1989. Since then, the FICO score has become the most widely used credit scoring system by lenders and financial institutions to evaluate a consumer's credit risk.

The Smart Home Buyer

FICO Score Components and Calculation

FICO scores range from 300 to 850 and are calculated using five factors:

- Payment history (35%): This component considers your record of timely payments on credit accounts, such as credit cards, loans, and mortgages. Late or missed payments can significantly lower your score.

- Amounts owed (30%): This factor assesses the total amount of debt you owe and the proportion of available credit you are using (credit utilization). High balances or high credit utilization can negatively impact your score, as they may indicate over-reliance on credit.

- Length of credit history (15%): This component evaluates the age of your oldest credit account, the average age of all your accounts, and the age of individual accounts. A longer credit history generally results in a higher score, as it demonstrates a longer track record of responsible credit management.

- Credit mix (10%): This factor considers the variety of credit types you have, including credit cards, installment loans, and mortgages. A diverse credit portfolio can positively impact your score, as it demonstrates your ability to manage different types of credit.

- New credit (10%): This component takes into account the number of recent credit inquiries and newly opened credit accounts. Multiple inquiries or opening several new accounts in a short period may signal financial distress, which can lower your score.

FICO Score Models

FICO has released several credit scoring models over the years. The algorithm is refined in order to improve predictive accuracy. Some of the most notable FICO scoring models include:

- FICO Score 8: Introduced in 2009, FICO Score 8 is the most widely used version of the FICO score. It places a higher emphasis on high credit card utilization, penalizes isolated late payments more severely, and ignores small-dollar "nuisance" collection accounts (less than $100). It also has a more lenient approach towards rate-shopping inquiries, treating multiple inquiries for the same type of credit within a 45-day window as a single inquiry.

- FICO Score 9: Launched in 2014, FICO Score 9 further refines the scoring model by excluding paid collection accounts and reducing the impact of unpaid medical collections. It also incorporates rental payment history when available, making the model more inclusive for consumers with limited or non-traditional credit histories.

- Industry-specific FICO scores: FICO also offers industry-specific scoring models tailored to specific types of credit, such as auto loans, credit cards, and mortgages. These models consider the unique risk factors associated with each type of credit and may generate different scores than the base FICO model. Examples include the FICO Auto Score and the FICO Bankcard Score.

FICO Scores and Mortgage Lending

Mortgage lenders often use older FICO scoring models when evaluating applicants for home loans. The most common models used for mortgage lending are:

1. FICO Score 2 (Experian)
2. FICO Score 4 (TransUnion)
3. FICO Score 5 (Equifax)

These models are also referred to as "Classic FICO" or "FICO Rescore" and were specifically tailored to analyze and predict mortgage risk. While their algorithms are similar to FICO Score 8, they, in most instances, produce slightly different scores due to variations in the treatment of certain factors such as inquiries, credit utilization, and late payments.

Mortgage lenders usually consider all three scores from the major credit bureaus and use the middle score to determine your eligibility and loan terms. This is known as a "tri-merge" or "merged credit report.

VantageScore

VantageScore is a credit scoring model developed as a joint venture by the three major credit bureaus: Equifax, Experian, and TransUnion. Launched in 2006, VantageScore was designed to provide a more consistent and accurate assessment of an individual's creditworthiness across the three credit bureaus. Since then, it has been updated several times, with VantageScore 4.0 being the most recent iteration.

VantageScore Components and Calculation

VantageScore takes into account several factors to calculate a credit score, which ranges from 300 to 850. The model considers the following components:

- Payment history (41%): This factor examines your history of timely payments on credit accounts, including credit cards, loans, and mortgages. Late or missed payments can significantly lower your score.
- Age and type of credit (20%): This component evaluates the age of your oldest credit account and the average age of all your accounts. It also considers the mix of credit types you have, such as installment loans, credit cards, and mortgages. A diverse credit portfolio with a longer history can positively impact your score.

- Credit utilization (20%): This factor assesses the ratio of your credit balances to your credit limits. High utilization rates can indicate that you're over-relying on credit, which may negatively affect your score. It's generally recommended to keep your credit utilization below 30%.

- Balances (11%): This component takes into account the total amount of debt you owe across all your credit accounts. High balances, especially on revolving credit lines like credit cards, can lower your score.

- Recent credit behavior and inquiries (5%): This factor considers the number of recent hard inquiries on your credit report and the opening of new credit accounts. Frequent inquiries and opening multiple new accounts in a short period may signal financial distress, which can lower your score.

- Available credit (3%): This component looks at the amount of unused credit available to you. Having more available credit can be a positive factor, as it indicates that you are managing your credit responsibly.

VantageScore 4.0: Introduced in 2017, VantageScore 4.0 is the latest version of the model and incorporates advanced machine learning techniques to improve its predictive accuracy. This version places a greater emphasis on trended credit data, which analyzes credit behavior over time rather than relying solely on a snapshot of a consumer's credit profile. By considering trended data, VantageScore 4.0 can better identify consumers who are improving or declining in creditworthiness.

In addition to using trended data, VantageScore 4.0 addresses the issue of "sparse credit files" by leveraging alternative data sources, such as rental payment history and utility bill payments, to generate scores for consumers with limited or no traditional credit history. This makes the model more inclusive and expands access to credit for a broader range of consumers.

The Smart Home Buyer

VantageScore vs. FICO Score

While VantageScore and FICO are both credit scoring models, there are some key differences between the two:

- Score range: Both VantageScore and FICO scores range from 300 to 850. However, the weighting of factors and the algorithm used to calculate scores may differ, leading to potential variations in the scores provided by each model.

- Scoring factors: VantageScore and FICO use similar factors to determine credit scores but assign different weights to these factors. For example, VantageScore places more emphasis on payment history and credit utilization, while FICO places a higher weight on amounts owed and the length of credit history.

- Credit history requirements: VantageScore requires a shorter credit history for generating a score. It can produce a credit score for individuals with as little as one month of credit history or one account reported within the past two years. In contrast, FICO requires at least six months of credit history and at least one account reported within the past six months.

- Treatment of late payments: VantageScore is more lenient with late payments on isolated accounts, while FICO is less forgiving. If you have a strong overall credit history but one account with late payments, your VantageScore may be less affected than your FICO score.

- Treatment of inquiries: VantageScore has a longer de-duplication window for rate-shopping inquiries. This means that multiple inquiries for the same type of credit within a 14-day window are treated as a single inquiry, minimizing the impact on your score. FICO has a shorter window of 45 days for some credit types, such as mortgages and auto loans.

Marc Saint Clair, MBA

Tips:

Improving your FICO score will help you secure better loan terms, lower rates, and, overall, more credit options.

- Make a concerted effort to remove and clear all accounts in collections.

- Always pay your bills on time, as late payments have a negative impact on your score. Payment history is the most significant factor in your FICO score.

- Maintain credit utilization low. Keep all your credit cards below 30% of the maximum allowable limit.

- Maintain a diverse credit mix: Having a variety of credit types, such as credit cards, installment loans, and mortgages, demonstrates your ability to manage different types of credit.

- Limit inquiries. Do not open any new credit lines before or during the loan application process. This is important because checking your credit with a low score will further lower your score and reduce your chances of obtaining a good interest rate.

- Check all three credit reports regularly for errors and request removal of errors from the respective credit bureau. Fixing errors is a common tool used by credit repair companies to help their customers improve their scores significantly overnight.

- Not all credit-building solutions on the market will improve your credit.

- Most online services that provide you with your credit score do not actually use the version for the mortgage. As such, your lender-reported credit score for your loan application might be different.

The Smart Home Buyer

How to start building credit if you have no credit history

- Get a secured credit card at your local bank. You can start with as little as $100.
- Get a store card. However, make sure to ask them if they report to the credit bureau.
- Become an authorized user on another person's credit card.

Marc Saint Clair, MBA

Chapter 5
Mortgages & Down Payment Requirements

A mortgage is a legal agreement between you, the borrower, and a lender (bank or creditor). In this agreement you promise to make payments on time, and if you fail to repay, you agree for the lender to take the property.

How much do I need to put down?

The amount of down payment required varies chiefly by the mortgage package that you are getting. In order to get a mortgage, you will need a mortgage broker to help you identify which mortgage you qualify for. We are going to go over the different types of mortgages that you will come across and the down payment requirements for each one. By understanding these various loans, you will be able to make informed decisions when selecting a mortgage that aligns with your financial goals and circumstances. Regulations and guidelines change periodically. The information below will help provide a general guide for the current market.

Here are a few essential terms you might come across.

Down payment:

Down payment is a percentage of the loan that the lender requires that you provide at the time of closing. Most loans have a down payment requirement. If you are required to put 3.5% down for your mortgage, this means that by the time of closing, 3.5% of the funds going to the seller will come from you, and the other 96.5% will come from the bank.

The Smart Home Buyer

Mortgage Insurance:

Private Mortgage Insurance (PMI) or Mortgage Insurance Premium (MIP) is a mortgage insurance that you may be required to pay as a condition of getting a loan. Mortgage insurance protects only the lender if you stop making payments on your loan. It can be a one-time upfront fee at closing or a monthly payment obligation that you make along with your mortgage. Most loan packages have both an upfront fee and a monthly fee.

Gift Funds:

Borrowers can use gift funds from family and friends to cover down payment and closing cost expenses. Guidelines vary from loan to loan. Generally, a "gift" letter will be required from the donor that will indicate that the money is a gift and is not expected to be repaid. Additionally, the letter will require the following:

  a. Donors' information.
  b. Relationship to the borrower.
  c. Source of the gift.
  d. both the donor's and recipient's signatures.
  e. Information about the donation amount.

The lender will need to source the money. Sourcing the money involves requiring the donor to provide one or more documents, including signed affidavits, bank statements, copies of cashed checks, proof of electronic transfers, and proof of original balance from the donor's bank account. Any gift over $17,000 to a person will require filing a gift tax return to the IRS.

Loan to Value LTV:

Loan to Value calculates how much the amount borrowed compares to the value of the house. This helps them determine how much risk they're taking with the loan. The lower the LTV, the better. The bullseye LTV ratio for most lenders is 80%. Eighty percent of LTV means that you were able to put down 20%. Anything higher will generally require mortgage insurance.

Fixed-rate mortgage:

Fixed-rate mortgages are loans that have a specific interest rate for the duration of the loan.

Adjustable-rate mortgage (ARM):

Adjustable-rate mortgages are home loans that have an interest rate that adjusts based on the market interest rate. It is broken into two periods. The first is a fixed period that usually lasts between 5-10 years, where the interest rate won't change. The second is the adjustment period where your interest rate can go up or down based on the market rate.

Conforming Loans:

Conforming loans are loans that meet certain guidelines where the lender can sell these loans to government-sponsored entities such as Fannie Mae, Freddie Mac, and the Federal Housing Finance Agency for repackaging after closing. It is very common for you to receive a notice that indicates that your loan has been sold to another entity within a few months after closing.

Non-Conforming Loans:

Non-conforming loans cannot be sold to government-sponsored entities after closing.

The Smart Home Buyer

Loan Estimate (Closing disclosures):

The loan estimate will have a line-by-line price range for every potential expense you might have to make during the due diligence process of purchase. Under the Truth and Lending Act, a loan estimation is required from the lender to the borrower in order to inform them of any and all potential fees associated with obtaining the loan.

Front-End DTI:

Front-end DTI is a debt-to-income ratio that calculates the percentage of your gross income that is going toward your mortgage. It considers your PITI (Principal, Interest, Taxes, and Insurance) for DTI ratio calculation. The lower the ratio, the better.

Back-End DTI:

Back-end DTI is a debt-to-income ratio that calculates the percentage of your gross income going toward all debt, such as principal, interest, taxes, insurance, car loans, credit cards, child support, student loans, and any other loans.

It is calculated by adding your total monthly debt expense divided by your monthly gross income and dividing the result by 100. Some lenders only take into account the back-end DTI. The lower the ratio, the better.

Here is what you can do to decrease your DTI:

1. Increase your income.
2. Decrease debt.
3. Decrease your mortgage payment.

Marc Saint Clair, MBA

Types of loan

This is a general overview of the current market situation. Some lenders are more flexible while others are more stringent on the requirements listed.

FHA (Federal Housing Administration)

A FHA loan is a mortgage that is insured by the federal government. FHA loans are ideal for buyers who have a lower credit score and higher debt-to-income ratio. It also allows for a lower down payment.

Credit Score Minimum: 580

Minimum Down payment: 3.5% of the purchase price for credit scores 580 and above. Down payment requirement is higher for credit scores of 500-579.

Mortgage Insurance & Fees: FHA loans don't have private mortgage insurance (PMI). They do, however, have something somewhat similar to a PMI called an up-front mortgage insurance premium (UFMIP) and a mortgage insurance premium (MIP). The upfront mortgage insurance premium is equal to 1.75% of the loan, and it is paid at closing. The mortgage insurance premium is paid monthly for either 11 years if you put down at least 10% or the lifetime of the mortgage if you put less than 10% down. In general, as you make payments, your MIP decreases every year.

Debt to income ratio: Front end 29, Back end 43%, max

Gifts Toward Closing: Can receive gifts from family members and really close friends up to the down payment and closing cost amount.

Occupancy Type: Primary Residence; Must occupy within 60 days of the closing.

Residence Type: Single-family to-four-unit home

Other Requirement: No cash reserve requirement for one-to-two-unit properties. Three or more-unit properties require cash reserve.

Fun Fact:

Before 2013, MIP would be canceled automatically the minute that the borrower has 20% equity in their home.

TIPS:

While you cannot entirely avoid MIP in your FHA loan, you can, however reduce it by putting down 10%. By doing that, you will stop paying MIP after 11 years.

Refinance to a conventional loan once you reach 20% equity.

Conventional

Conventional mortgages are loans that are not backed by a government agency. They vary widely in size and scope. Conventional loans are the most popular mortgage option on the market.

Credit Score Minimum: 620

Minimum Down Payment: 3%

Mortgage Insurance & Fees: If you put down less than 20% on a conventional loan, you will need to make monthly PMI payments. There are no upfront PMIs to be paid at closing. The higher your credit score and down payment, the lower your PMI.

PMI is more expensive than MIP.

Debt to Income Ratio: Front end 31%, back end 45% Max, slightly higher DTI with higher credit score.

Gifts Toward Closing: Only family and extended family members can gift.

Occupancy Type: Primary Residence, rental, second home, and

Marc Saint Clair, MBA

other.

<u>Residence Type</u>: Single-family to four-unit home

<u>Other Requirement</u>: Cash reserve requirement varies.

Fun Fact:

Once you reach 22% equity in your home, your PMI is automatically canceled.

TIPS:

If you can afford a little more on your monthly mortgage payment, consider a 15-year loan. You will pay less in interest for the life of the loan. Alternatively, if you can make a second payment on your mortgage every month or periodically, it will go a long way to help you achieve that 22%. When you send the second payment, it has to be separate from the first payment. <u>You must write on the check that it is to be applied only toward the principal</u>.

USDA

USDA mortgages are loans that are guaranteed by the US Department of Agriculture (USDA). They are designed to help low to moderate-income home buyers purchase homes in rural areas.

<u>Credit Score Minimum</u>: 640

<u>Minimum Down Payment</u>: 0%

<u>Mortgage Insurance & Fees</u>: Upfront guarantee fee of 1% plus an annual fee of 0.35% of the loan amount calculated each year.

<u>Debt to Income Ratio</u>: Back end 41% Maximum. Slightly higher DTI with a higher credit score.

<u>Gifts Toward Closing</u>: Anyone not benefiting from a buyer buying the home can get a gift.

The Smart Home Buyer

<u>Occupancy Type</u>: Primary Residence

<u>Residence Type</u>: Single-family to three-unit home.

<u>Other Requirement</u>: No cash reserve requirement after closing unless you have a higher DTI. The income limit does apply.

Fun Fact:

Not restricted to only first-time home buyers.

The income of all working family members, including those not on the mortgage, is added to the income restriction calculation.

TIPS:

Square footage limitations range between 400-2,000 sq feet. So make sure that during your search when you search that your home falls within that square footage requirement.

VA

The US Department of Veterans Affairs (VA) provides home loans to veterans, active-duty personnel, and other serving military personnel.

<u>Credit Score Minimum</u>: 580 – 620. 620 is the lowest most VA-approved lenders will accept.

<u>Minimum Down Payment</u>: 0%

<u>Mortgage Insurance & Fees</u>: No mortgage insurance. However, it has a one-time VA funding fee average of 1% (Range from 0.5%-3.60%). Disabled vets and surviving spouses of veterans don't pay the funding fee.

<u>Debt to Income Ratio</u>: Back end 41% Maximum. Slightly higher DTI with a higher credit score.

<u>Gifts Toward Closing</u>: No limit. No seller cashback limit.

Marc Saint Clair, MBA

<u>Occupancy Type</u>: Primary Residence

<u>Residence Type</u>: Single-family to Four unit home.

<u>Other Requirement</u>: Pest Inspection; appraisal can be waived if putting at least 20% down. No loan limits. No cash reserve requirement. Depending on your situation, the lender might require cash reserve.

Fun Fact:

Surviving spouses are eligible for VA loans.

TIPS:

- I have seen more loan rejections from VA banks in comparison to independent VA approved lenders. In a nutshell, if your application is on the border line, you might have more success with an independently approved VA lender rather than the VA credit union where you bank.

- Request a certificate of eligibility (COE) before contacting a mortgage broker for a VA loan.

https://www.va.gov/housing-assistance/home-loans/how-to-request-coe/

Jumbo Loan

Jumbo loans are mortgages that are used to facilitate the purchase of homes that exceed the price limit of a conforming loan. The maximum about you can borrow in 2023 for a single-family in most parts of the US is $726,200. Jumbo loans are not backed by any government agency and cannot be sold to government-sponsored entities such as Fannie Mae, Freddie Mac, or the Federal Housing Finance Agency for repackaging.

The Smart Home Buyer

<u>Credit Score Minimum</u>: 700+

<u>Minimum Down Payment</u>: 10-20%

<u>Mortgage Insurance & Fees</u>: PMI if under 20% down.

<u>Debt to Income Ratio</u>: 45% Max

<u>Gifts Toward Closing</u>: Yes

<u>Occupancy Type</u>: Primary, secondary, vacation, and investment property.

<u>Residence Type</u>: Single-family and multi-family.

<u>Other Requirement</u>: Cash reserve varies according to borrower profile.

Fun Fact:

It is commonly used to finance luxury properties in high-income areas

The VA also offers Jumbo Loans. You can only buy a primary residence with it, though.

TIPS:

- If you are not able to save enough for a Jumbo loan. You can get an 80-10-10 Piggyback loan. 80-10-10 piggyback loan is broken down accordingly: First Mortgage - Second Mortgage - Down Payment.

Hard Money Loan

Hard money loan is a short-term loan that is secured by the property that the buyer is buying. The lenders are usually companies or individuals. While hard money is faster to obtain with less credit requirements, it is very expensive. A borrower can close on a hard money loan in as little as 10 days. Nevertheless, rates are, on average, 4-15% higher than traditional mortgage rates.

Marc Saint Clair, MBA

<u>Credit Score Minimum</u>: Credit scores are often not a major factor in getting a hard money loan.

<u>Minimum Down Payment</u>: 25-35%

<u>Mortgage Insurance & Fees</u>: Upfront fees and closing costs are expected.

<u>Debt to Income Ratio</u>: Not a major factor.

<u>Gifts Toward Closing</u>: Not a major factor.

<u>Occupancy Type</u>: They generally prefer not to fund owner-occupied residences.

<u>Residence Type</u>: Single-family, multi-family, building, commercial real estate.

<u>Other Requirement</u>: Real estate knowledge. Most hard money lenders are curious about your real estate background. If you have no real estate experience, they will shy away from lending.

Fun Fact:

Hard money loans are mostly based on the value of the property rather than the creditworthiness of the borrower. Therefore, the application process is less extensive.

TIPS:

If you are flipping a house, make sure that you plan accordingly to make payments on time. Missed payments are very costly.

Construction loan

Construction loan is a short-term loan that is used to buy land and or finance the renovation or construction of a residential or commercial property. Funds are provided in stages (draws) of the construction.

The Smart Home Buyer

There are two general ways of doing a construction loan.

a. <u>Construction only mortgage</u> is financing only the construction of the property. Once you complete your construction, you will require a long-term loan. That is why most builders sell the property before it is completed. If the property is completed, it will require another long-term loan.

b. <u>Construction to permanent loan</u> is both a construction mortgage and a long-term mortgage in one. You only do one closing for the construction and long-term mortgage. This is ideal for an owner-occupied property. The rate is locked from the onset for both loans.

<u>Credit Score Minimum</u>: 620 or higher

<u>Minimum Down Payment</u>: 20% or more

<u>Mortgage Insurance & Fees</u>: If down payment is less than 20% of the appraised value.

<u>Debt to Income Ratio</u>: 43% or lower.

<u>Gifts Toward Closing</u>: Yes, For some lenders, at least 5% of the down payment cannot be a gift.

<u>Occupancy Type</u>: Residential, Investment.

<u>Residence Type</u>: Single-family, Multi-family, Commercial.

<u>Other Requirements</u>: Builder and construction plans and a qualified builder, among other things.

Fun Fact: You will only pay interest on the actual amount borrowed. Given that the borrower will borrow in draws, you don't pay interest on the total amount to be borrowed but rather only on the amount that was drawn.

TIPS:

Marc Saint Clair, MBA

Be well acquainted with the payment terms, disbursement process, and all the necessary hurdles before beginning your construction project.

Rehab Loan

Rehab loan, also known as a renovation loan, is a loan that is designed to both purchase and rehabilitate or renovate a property. Rehab loans are used to buy fixer-uppers that need significant repairs. While homeowners can tap into a home equity line of credit (HELOC) to rehab their property, the rehab loans we will talk about in this book will be for the purpose of buying and repairing.

FHA 203K Rehab Loan

There are two types:

Limited 203K rehab loan for minor repairs. No structural work. A HUD consultant is not required.

203K rehab loan is for major repairs over $35,000. A HUD-accepted consultant is required.

Credit Score Minimum: 580 or higher.

Minimum Down Payment: 3.5-5%

Mortgage Insurance & Fees: Both upfront and monthly. Less if more than 10% down.

Debt to Income Ratio: 43% max.

Gifts Toward Closing: Yes, flexible. 100% of the down payment can be gift-funded.

Occupancy Type: Primary residence

Residence Type: Single-family and multi-family.

The Smart Home Buyer

<u>Other Requirement</u>: Must have a HUD consultant to help you manage bids from contractors.

<u>Fun Facts</u>: 203K Rehab loan Can be used for structural issues and for reconstruction.

HUD consultants inspect the property, consult on repair plans, consult on the cost of repairs, manage the project and provide a work workup. There is a fee for the consultant.

When using a consultant, the steps are as follows:

1. Get Preapproved.
2. Make offers on properties located in USDA-approved locations.
3. Offer is accepted, and the property is under contract.
4. Identify a HUD-accepted consultant to work with.
5. Initial consultation and feasibility study with the consultant to discuss renovation plans.
6. Obtain bids from contractors and work on repair cost estimates.
7. Review contractor bids & Hire a contractor.
8. Complete loan application.
9. Obtain commitment letter.
10. Close to the property.
11. Start work
12. The repairs will be broken up into multiple parts. The consultant will release funds in tranches. Every time one or more parts are done, the consultant visits and approves the release of funds. This process continues until all the parts of the rehab are completed.
13. Project closeout.

Marc Saint Clair, MBA

VA Renovation Loan

Credit Score Minimum: 620

Minimum Down Payment: $0. Yes, Zero.

Mortgage Insurance & Fees: Yes, Funding fee. Varies with a degree of service.

Debt to Income Ratio: 41% or less.

Gifts Toward Closing: Yes, flexible

Occupancy Type: Owner-occupied

Residence Type: Single-family, Multi-family.

Fannie Mae HomeStyle Renovation Loan

Credit Score Minimum: 620 or higher

Minimum Down Payment: 5%

Mortgage Insurance & Fees: if less than 20% PMI is required.

Debt to Income Ratio: 43% max

Gifts Toward Closing: Yes, flexible

Occupancy Type: Primary residence, second home, and investment property.

Residence Type: Single-family and multifamily.

Fun Fact: You can use the Fannie Mae Homestyle Renovation Loan as an investor.

Freddie Mac CHOICE Renovation Loan

CHOICEreno eXPress for small-scale renovations.

CHOICE Renovation Loan is for larger and more extensive projects.

The Smart Home Buyer

<u>Credit Score Minimum</u>: 620 or higher

<u>Minimum Down Payment</u>: As low as 3% for eligible borrowers. Generally 5-20%.

<u>Mortgage Insurance & Fees</u>: Yes

<u>Debt to Income Ratio</u>: 43 Maximum

<u>Gifts Toward Closing</u>: Gift is allowed.

<u>Occupancy Type</u>: Primary residence, one unit second home, and one unit investment properties.

<u>Residence Type</u>: Single-family up to four-unit primary residence.

<u>Other Requirement</u>: Require an escrow account that will have renovation funds, contingency funds and up to six months of mortgage. The funds will be held until closing.

<u>Fun Fact</u>: Loan terms can be 15, 20, or 30 years. It can be used for condominiums in approved areas. This is a single mortgage for renovation and long-term. Rates are lower compared to other lenders. Available for existing home owners that want to renovate homes as well as home buyers.

USDA Renovation Loan

<u>USDA Limited</u> allows for financing up to $35,000 in repairs for non-structural renovations.

<u>USDA Standard</u> allows for financing that exceeds $35,000 for structural and cosmetic issues.

<u>Credit Score Minimum</u>: 620

<u>Minimum Down Payment</u>: Zero down payment.

<u>Mortgage Insurance & Fees</u>: Upfront guarantee fee plus monthly fee rolled into a mortgage.

<u>Debt to Income Ratio</u>: Back end 41% Maximum

<u>Gifts Toward Closing</u>: Seller can contribute up to 6% toward the

closing cost of the buyer.

Occupancy Type: Primary residence

Residence Type: Single Family and modular home. (No multi-family – 2-4 units)

Other Requirement: Property must be located in a rural or suburban area. Income limits do apply. Requires a HUD consultant. A 10-15% contingency fee is required in case the renovation runs over. 10% if utilities are turned on. 15% if utilities are not turned off.

Fun Fact: Property must be at least one year old. It can't be used to add a new swimming pool.

DSCR Loan (Debt Service Coverage Ratio Loan)

A Debt Service Coverage Ratio (DSCR) loan is a type of financing primarily used for income-generating properties such as rental properties, commercial buildings, or multifamily units. Unlike traditional mortgages, which rely heavily on the borrower's credit score and income, DSCR loans focus more on the property's ability to generate sufficient cash flow to cover the loan payments. Lenders assess the property's income potential and evaluate its Debt Service Coverage Ratio, which measures the property's ability to cover its debt obligations. DSCR loans are often favored by real estate investors looking to acquire properties that can generate consistent rental income.

Credit Score Minimum: 575

Minimum Down Payment: 20% on average. 10% based on other factors.

Mortgage Insurance & Fees: Usually, no mortgage insurance is required, but fees may vary by lender.

Debt to Income Ratio: Typically not specified, but lenders assess borrower's ability to cover debt obligations.

The Smart Home Buyer

<u>Gifts Toward Closing</u>: Varies by lender.

<u>Occupancy Type</u>: Can be used for investment properties or commercial real estate.

<u>Residence Type</u>: Income-generating properties: rental properties, commercial buildings, or multifamily units.

<u>Other Requirement</u>: Lenders may require documentation of rental income or cash flow from the property.

<u>Fun Fact</u>: DSCR loans are primarily used by real estate investors to finance income-producing properties and are evaluated based on the property's ability to generate sufficient cash flow to cover the loan payments.

Foreign National Loan (Requirements vary from lender to lender)

Some lenders will lend to you if you are living in the US temporarily, while others require that you live outside of the US.

<u>Credit Score Minimum</u>: No US credit is required. Some might require credit from your country of origin.

<u>Minimum Down Payment</u>: Typically ranges from 20% to 50%.

<u>Mortgage Insurance & Fees</u>: Usually, when you put 20% down or more, there is no need for mortgage insurance. However, some lenders might impose additional fees.

<u>Debt to Income Ratio</u>: Specified by most lenders.

<u>Gifts Toward Closing</u>: Varies by lender.

<u>Occupancy Type</u>: Can be used for primary residence, second home, or investment property.

<u>Residence Type</u>: Eligible for single-family homes, townhouses, condos, and 2-4-unit properties.

<u>Other Requirements</u>: No social security number, no green card, no

visa, and no US credit score needed. Must demonstrate income stability and ability to repay. Some lenders might require multi-month mortgage payment reserves. You will be required to have an ITIN number.

Fun Fact: Foreign national loans usually require more paperwork than conventional loans.

ITIN Loan

Credit Score Minimum: 620

Minimum Down Payment: 15% - 30%

Mortgage Insurance & Fees: Usually, when you put 20% down or more, there is no mortgage insurance. Some lenders might have additional fees.

Debt to Income Ratio: Specified by most lenders.

Gifts Toward Closing: Varies by lender.

Occupancy Type: Varies by lender.

Residence Type: Varies by the lender (Single Family, townhouse, condo, 2-4 Unit homes).

Other Requirement: Must have a valid ITIN number, Passport from country of origin.

Fun Fact: This home loan is for people who do not have a social security number. Immigration status does not affect someone to get an ITIN mortgage.

**Step Two
Start The Search**

Chapter 6
Pre-approval letter

To find out how much you are qualified to spend on a House, you will need to visit a mortgage broker and obtain a pre-approval letter. Contacting a mortgage broker will officially kick off your effort to buy a home.

A mortgage broker will collect information from you, such as your income and debt information, among other things. The broker will figure out what is the best loan package for you. There are many different loan packages. Some lenders might have more loan programs than others. After you meet with a mortgage broker, the outcome will result in one of the following:

- The mortgage broker will issue you a preapproval based on your economic strength or
- The mortgage broker will ask you to fix one or more items and come back.

The following documents are required for obtaining a pre-approval:

- Two recent pay stubs or pay statements
- Two consecutive years of W2 and/or 1099 forms
- Two recent tax returns
- Three most recent bank statements

Typically, once the mortgage broker receives all of the necessary documents, the broker can produce a pre-approval letter within five business days. If you are self-employed, you will need a minimum of three years' worth of income documentation.

How to pick a Mortgage Broker

Ask friends and acquaintances who recently purchased a home for a referral. Given that things change over time, it is important to get feedback from recent home buyers. It is good to start with at least two mortgage brokers and work with the one who answers your calls and gives you a good deal.

First-time home buyer class

Some lenders might require that you take a first-time home buyer class. As long as the class certificate is in hand before underwriting, you should be fine.

Down payment assistance

Cities, towns, and lenders often times have down payment assistance available. It is good to connect with different lenders such as credit unions and another type of bank, because they don't always have access to the same type of loan products and grants. That is why it is good to apply and have your credit pulled in the same week by more than one lender.

Tips:

- Before contacting a mortgage broker, make sure to have all required documents ready.
- Avoid moving large amounts of money in and out of your bank account, as it will show on your recent bank statements. If you must move a significant sum of money, be prepared to provide evidence of the origin and purpose of the funds.
- Consider shopping around and obtaining pre-approval letters from more than one lender. It's recommended to obtain pre-approval letters from up to two lenders so they can run your credit around the same time, as it doesn't negatively impact your credit score, even if it's below 700. Keep in mind that interest rates for the same type of loan may vary from lender

Marc Saint Clair, MBA

to lender. It's a good idea to compare offers from large commercial banks, small banks, and credit unions, as they tend to be more competitive.

Chapter 7
Real Estate Representation

Types of Representation

Buyer Agent – Buyer agents and their brokerage firm provide the highest standard of care and service to the buyer, working exclusively for the buyer's financial interest.

Seller Agent – Seller agents and their brokerage firm represent the seller and the seller's financial interest while providing high-quality service.

Dual Agent – When a single real estate agent represents both the buyer and the seller in the same transaction, they become a dual agent. This type of agent owes confidentiality to both parties and may face limitations in providing insightful advice to each other due to confidentiality constraints.

Designated Agent – When the buyer and seller are represented by different agents within the same brokerage firm, they are working with designated agents.

The Importance of a Buyer Agent

Working with a knowledgeable and effective buyer agent is highly valuable. For first-time homebuyers, it is crucial to have an experienced, client-focused agent to guide you through the process. If you are a repeat buyer, you need an agent who will fight for your interests and negotiate every detail. However, not all agents are equally effective. Some may be more proactive, while others may be indifferent or disinterested in the client's needs. This can be due to factors such as low commission potential, burnout from repetitive processes, personal dislike of the buyer, or a buyer's unrealistic expectations based on current market conditions.

Marc Saint Clair, MBA

The Role of a Buyer Agent:
1. Buffer
2. Guide
3. Educator
4. Resource

Buffer

When buying a home, there are a lot of emotions and negotiations involved between the buyer and the seller. Sellers can have unrealistic expectations about the value of their home, which can make the process difficult for buyers. A good buyer agent acts as a buffer, filtering out the emotions and unclear language to give the buyer a clear understanding of the seller's position and objective. This allows the buyer to make informed decisions free from negative influence.

Lesson Learned:

Buffers Keep Deals on Track to Close

One of my first clients as a real estate agent was Edgar. We viewed various properties and eventually settled on a home that was suitable for him and his family. The sellers informed Edgar that they would be taking the stainless-steel refrigerator with them but would replace it with another refrigerator before the closing date. Initially, the offer was accepted with the condition that all appliances remain on the premises. However, during the counteroffer process, the sellers verbally agreed to exchange the appliance. Edgar was content with this arrangement as he was pleased with the property.

However, during the final walk-through, just two days before closing, Edgar discovered that the new fridge was used and of inferior quality and did not match with the other appliances in the kitchen. He became frustrated and informed the seller that he

The Smart Home Buyer

wouldn't close unless they fulfilled their part of the agreement. The seller argued that they had kept their end of the bargain by replacing the refrigerator.

Edgar realized that had he known the seller's intent, he wouldn't have agreed to move forward with buying the property. This caused a 24-hour delay in the closing process. On the day before closing, I reached out to the seller's agent to find out if the seller would be willing to compromise. The seller's agent said "no". I did some research and found that the appliance that was in the House during the initial showing was on sale for $900 at a local retail store. Both parties were willing to walk away from the deal. I asked the seller's agent if he would be willing to split the cost with me, at $450 each, to close the deal. The seller's agent agreed, and we were able to save the deal.

In the end, both the seller and buyer were happy with the outcome, even though they did not speak to each other during the closing. To avoid similar surprises in the future, I advise putting in writing that the replaced appliance must match the other appliances or have the desired quality.

Guide

A buyer agent acts as a guide to a House buyer by providing expert guidance and support throughout the entire home-buying process. The agent helps the buyer navigate the complex world of real estate and provides them with important information and insights that they might not have access to otherwise. This includes things like market trends, current home prices, and the availability of homes that meet the buyer's specific needs and preferences.

The buyer agent also acts as a liaison between the buyer and the seller, helping to communicate the buyer's needs and wants and negotiating the best possible deal for the buyer. This might involve negotiating the price, closing costs, and other important details of the sale.

Marc Saint Clair, MBA

Additionally, the buyer agent is there to answer any questions the buyer may have and provide them with the guidance and support they need to make informed decisions. This might include discussing the pros and cons of different homes, helping the buyer understand the home buying process, and providing them with information about the local real estate market and the House market specifically.

Lesson learned:

I recall working with a buyer named Victor during a housing market boom in 2015. Despite being outbid on 15 previous offers, I showed him over 50 properties over a 9-month period. Finally, we found a property that had almost everything he was looking for, and he placed an offer of $4,000 above the asking price. The offer was accepted without a counteroffer.

However, after the home inspection, Victor became concerned about some minor issues with the property. He wanted to use the inspection report as leverage to renegotiate a lower price and demanded that the seller fix all the issues. The seller agreed to fix about 40% of them, but Victor was unhappy with the remaining issues, which would cost around $600 to repair. I advised Victor that some sellers may refuse to fix anything, while others may only fix a portion, and that the seller, in this case, had agreed to fix half of the issues.

Despite this, Victor was still not satisfied and wanted the remaining issues resolved before closing. I understand his position, but I also pointed out that it was possible to request a return of his deposit and resume the search if the seller was not willing to budge.

At this point, Victor had a realization that he was potentially losing the perfect House over just $600. The Buyer Agent can play a crucial role in helping buyers navigate these types of challenges and make informed decisions.

The Smart Home Buyer

Educator

The process of buying a home, especially for the first time, can be overwhelming and challenging. A seasoned Buyer Agent can act as an educator to answer any questions the buyer may have and provide them with the guidance and support they need to make informed decisions.

One issue you may encounter is "buyer's remorse." This occurs when you start to second-guess your decision to buy a property, whether due to factors you didn't consider before making the offer or simply because you are imagining yourself living there. Your Buyer Agent can help you stay focused on your original goals and objectives and remind you why the current property is a good fit.

Lesson learned:

Laura, a first-time homebuyer, found her dream home but was concerned that the assessed value was significantly lower than the market value. Worried about making a bad investment, she reached out to me for advice.

I explained that the assessed value is primarily for tax purposes and often differs from the market value, which is based on recent comparable sales. Market value is determined by looking at the most recent three or more comparable sales—within a half-mile radius or more depending on the town's density—that have similar features, such as bedrooms, square footage, age, and updates. The average price of these comparable sales gives a more accurate reflection of the property's current worth.

After hearing this, Laura felt much more confident about her purchase. Understanding that market value reflects real-time demand and conditions, she proceeded with the transaction and was able to close the deal with peace of mind.

Marc Saint Clair, MBA

Resource

I have been working with a client, whom we'll call Rosa, for about five years. During this time, we started the home search process several times but had to halt it due to changes in Rosa's situation. However, after she got married, she reached out to me again to resume her search efforts. Initially, her husband wanted to work with another agent, but Rosa would still reach out to me for help in identifying potential homes or running comps on properties they liked. I respected the other agents and encouraged Rosa to continue working with them. However, after several failed attempts at finding a home with the other agent, Rosa and her husband decided to work exclusively with me. About a week later, they saw a property that was listed by the owner and asked me to place an offer on it. The seller accepted, but only under the condition that they wouldn't have to pay the buyer agent. I offered Rosa's husband a discounted rate, but they chose to go ahead with the deal without me in order to save on my 2% commission fee.

Unfortunately, this decision ended up costing them more in the long run. I knew of a similar loan program that I had advised one of my clients to switch to recently, which resulted in a lower upfront fee at closing and no mortgage insurance payments. While Rosa and her husband were able to save from a $6000 commission obligation, they ended up with a higher closing cost and extra monthly payments that added up to well over $30,000 on their property cost. It's important to remember that buyer agents are knowledgeable in deal structure, locations, mortgage packages, and other important aspects of buying a home. While you may have research and information from the internet, it's always better to have a formidable buyer agent by your side.

TIPS:

When interviewing real estate brokers, don't hesitate to inquire about the possibility of receiving funds from their commission to assist

The Smart Home Buyer

with your closing costs. Negotiating this aspect can potentially save you a significant amount of money. Many agents are open to providing a rebate of around $1,000 after closing, which can greatly alleviate the expenses associated with establishing your new home. Be proactive in discussing this option during your conversations with potential brokers, as it can make a substantial difference in your overall financial situation.

Marc Saint Clair, MBA

Chapter 8
Real Estate Attorney

Once your offer is accepted, the seller's side of the transaction will provide your side with a preliminary draft of the purchase and sales agreement for review. It is crucial to hire an attorney to carefully review this agreement. The buyer's side needs to thoroughly assess, make any necessary changes, and respond to counterchanges as required. This is where your real estate attorney becomes an invaluable asset.

When seeking a real estate attorney, it is essential to find one with experience in your region who is both affordable and personable. Real estate laws can be complex and can vary significantly from one region to another. You need an attorney who can scrutinize the Purchase and Sales agreement, ensuring that your interests are well-protected. A skilled attorney will also make sure you have reasonable contingency plans in place to address unexpected issues that could potentially jeopardize the deal or your earnest money deposit. While it's not mandatory, some buyers opt to have their attorney present at the closing for added peace of mind.

The bank involved in the transaction will also hire an attorney to oversee the closing process. The role of the bank's attorney is primarily to ensure that all the necessary paperwork is correctly completed and that all legal requirements are met. They are not there to take advantage of anyone but rather to ensure a smooth and legally compliant closing process. The cost of hiring the bank's attorney is typically included in your closing costs.

It is common practice for buyers to request that their attorney also represent the bank as the closing attorney. By doing so, buyers often receive a discount from their attorney for reviewing the purchase and sales agreement. If this approach is taken, your formal relationship with the attorney typically ends after the purchase and sales agreement review. However, you will have established a rapport that can facilitate future transactions.

The closing attorney, whether representing you or the bank, is responsible for handling all legal aspects of the closing process. This includes overseeing the title search and addressing any potential liens on the property. The goal is to ensure that the property is free from any encumbrances, such as liens or disputes, to facilitate a clear and undisputed transfer of ownership.

Marc Saint Clair, MBA

Step Three
Getting Your Property

Chapter 9
The Search

Finally, we've arrived at the exciting part! Now that you have a pre-approval in hand and a real estate salesperson to guide you let the search begin.

Clarify Your Priorities:

As you commence your search, it's essential to take note of and share with your real estate salesperson the attributes of your search, including your budget, preferred location, property type, and must-have features.

Consult with Your Mortgage Broker:

Consult with your mortgage broker to ensure that you are comfortable with the mortgage payment for the price and the area of your search.

Utilize Online Resources:

There are numerous ways you can independently search online. Most, if not all, of the platforms you will encounter are free to use. If you are working with an agent, they will subscribe you to a multiple listing system in their respective state. Unfortunately, while the information is more accurate, those multiple listing services are notorious for having a poor user interface.

Nevertheless, companies like Zillow, Trulia, Realtor.com, and many others obtain their data from your agent's multiple listing system. These companies, however, have better user interfaces.

Location is Crucial:

Location is crucial. Make sure that you are comfortable with the school system and the proximity to daily necessities such as grocery shopping, entertainment, and recreational activities.

What to Look for When Viewing a House:

A comprehensive home inspection conducted by a reputable and licensed home inspector is crucial before making the decision to proceed with the purchase and sales agreement after your offer is accepted. Nevertheless, during property showings, these are the factors you should pay attention to in order to better assess what you are getting into.

Outside the House:

Curb Appeal:

Curb appeal reflects the pride of ownership and serves as a preliminary indicator of how well the current homeowner or tenant maintains the property. If the property lacks curb appeal, it may be a sign that the property is not well maintained.

Exterior Walls:

- Vinyl Siding: Cost-effective, low maintenance, and resistant to pests and rot. However, it offers poor insulation and can be easily damaged by high-impact objects.
- Wood Siding: Provides desirable aesthetics but is comparatively more expensive and susceptible to pests.
- Fiber Cement: Low maintenance, durable, and resistant to pests, rot, and fire. However, it can be expensive and labor-intensive to install.

- Brick and Stone Veneer: Offer desirable aesthetics, durability, and decent insulation. Generally, more costly and requires significant effort for installation.
- Stucco Siding: Long-lasting and resistant to insects and fire but requires ongoing proactive maintenance.
- Metal Siding: Offers great looks, can mimic vinyl, and is durable, fire-resistant, and pest-resistant. However, it has poor insulation and can be noisy during rainfall.
- Composite Siding: Long-lasting, low maintenance, and resistant to pests and rot. Relatively more expensive than other types of sidings.

Roof:

Chimneys or exhaust systems are structures that provide passage for smoke, odor, gases, and combustion byproducts. They require a protective cover on top to prevent rain, animals, and debris from entering the house. You would commonly find them protruding through the roof or on the side of the roof. Chimneys with visible space between the bricks will require repointing as water could easily get between the bricks and cause water damage.

These are the common roofing materials found in the US:
- Asphalt Shingles: Asphalt shingles are affordable, low-maintenance, easy to install, and can last between 20 to 30 years. Some homeowners opt to add a second layer of asphalt roofing over the existing one to save time and money. This practice, known as "re-roofing," is not recommended. It can lead to increased costs during future roof replacements, reduced roof lifespan, and ventilation issues, among other issues. Fish mouths or shingle curling, which occur at the edges of shingles and resemble fish mouths, can cause roof leaks. Excess algae growth can also shorten the life of the

roof.

- Wood Shingles: Wood shingles are environmentally friendly, aesthetically pleasing, and can last for 30 to 50 years. However, they require regular maintenance and are susceptible to fire, rot, and wood-boring pests.

- Metal Roofing: Metal roofing is low-maintenance, energy-efficient, and can last over 50 years. However, it can be expensive and may produce noise during rain if not installed properly.

- Spanish Tiles: Spanish tiles are known for their aesthetic appeal, insulation properties, fire resistance, and low maintenance. They can last several decades. However, they are expensive and heavy, requiring a robust roofing structure. During wildfires, the embers can travel from one property to another, potentially causing fires. Homes with Spanish tiles are often less affected by such events.

- Slate Roofing: Slate roofing is the most durable option, with a lifespan of well over 100 years. It is commonly seen in Catholic churches. Slate roofs are resistant to fire, rot, and pests. However, the installation and repair of slate roofing can be extremely expensive due to the scarcity of qualified installers. Additionally, the material is heavy, sometimes necessitating additional structural support.

- Clay or Concrete Tiles: Clay or concrete tiles can last over 50 years or more and can mimic the appearance of other materials. They require regular maintenance and may necessitate roof structure reinforcement.

- Flat Roof Membrane: Flat roof membranes are commonly found on commercial and some residential properties. They are cost-effective and can last 20 to 25 years when properly installed.

- Green or Living Roofs: Green or living roofs are

environmentally friendly and improve insulation. However, they require highly specialized maintenance.

Water:

Houses typically receive their water supply from either city water or well water sources. Each source has its unique characteristics and considerations:

- City Water: City water is a commonly used water supply that undergoes treatment for quality and taste. It involves minimal maintenance for homeowners. However, it is advisable to install water filters in your house, as some cities may experience pipe issues or undetected chemical contaminants in the water supply.

- Well Water: Well water, on the other hand, originates from underground aquifers. Well systems require periodic maintenance and testing, and the need for treatment varies based on water quality. When purchasing a property with well water as the primary drinking water source, it is highly recommended to conduct water testing before finalizing the purchase. For instance, one of my clients recently had her well water tested and discovered elevated levels of radon and coliform bacteria, exceeding permissible limits. She negotiated with the seller to install a $3,700 mitigation system, safeguarding both her family's health and finances. Testing and addressing potential well water issues can result in significant benefits for homeowners.

Waste Elimination Systems:

In addition to water sources, homes are equipped with waste elimination systems to manage sewage and wastewater. The two most common options are city sewer systems and alternative waste methods:

- City Sewer System: City sewer systems are commonly used in urban and suburban areas. They are managed and maintained by municipal authorities, requiring little to no maintenance from homeowners.

- Septic Systems: In rural and less densely populated areas, septic systems are a common choice for waste elimination. Wastewater flows into the septic tank, where solids settle and are digested by bacteria. The treated wastewater then exits the tank and is dispersed into the drain field for further filtration and absorption into the ground. Septic systems require periodic maintenance.

- Alternative Waste Elimination Methods: In some cases, homes may utilize alternative waste elimination methods, such as composting toilets or incinerating toilets. These systems can be environmentally friendly and suitable for off-grid or eco-conscious homes. Composting toilets break down waste into compost that can be used as fertilizer while incinerating toilets burn waste to reduce it to ash.

Windows:

Modern windows often feature advanced technologies to improve energy efficiency and insulation. One such feature is the use of inert gases like argon or krypton between the window panes. These gases are inert and denser than air, reducing heat transfer and making homes more energy-efficient.

However, if you notice moisture buildup or condensation between the window panes, it may indicate a broken seal. The gas-filled space between the panes is sealed to prevent air and moisture from entering. A broken seal allows moisture infiltration, leading to foggy or hazy windows. This not only affects the window's insulation

The Smart Home Buyer

properties but also diminishes its clarity.

Inside the House:

The interior of a house is extensive and encompasses a wide range of considerations. I won't delve into these details here. Depending on your region, your home inspector will provide guidance on essential aspects, including but not limited to issues such as reverse polarity in electrical sockets and structural concerns.

My goal was to provide you with the main points to help you find your dream home. Every market is different, from the basement to the attic. As you see more and more properties, you will gain a better sense of what to look for as you proceed. Your home inspector will be able to inspect and provide insights into any issues.

Property Disclosure:

When you come across a property you're interested in; it's advisable to inquire with the seller's agent about the availability of a property disclosure. While not all properties have one, a property disclosure is a valuable document to review when considering making an offer. In it, the seller typically discloses pertinent information regarding the condition of the property. This disclosure can provide crucial insights into any known issues or concerns, helping you make a more informed decision about whether to proceed with an offer. Therefore, it's wise to request and thoroughly examine the property disclosure before moving forward in the home-buying process.

When you notice issues during a showing, there's no need to mention them to the seller's agent if you plan to conduct a home inspection. After the home inspection, you can negotiate the price or request necessary repairs. If you make the seller aware of these issues before making an offer, it may weaken your bargaining position.

Marc Saint Clair, MBA

Chapter 10
Condos

In this chapter, we'll delve into standard condos, a prevalent type of condominium arrangement where the primary structure is partitioned into individual units. Each unit encompasses everything within its walls, ceiling, and floor, and as a unit owner, you assume responsibility for the plumbing and wiring within your designated space. The common areas outside your unit, such as hallways, elevators, and shared amenities, are collectively owned by all condo residents. Let's explore the key features of standard condos.

Owner Occupied Only:

"Owner occupied only" or "100% owner occupied" condos are characterized by stringent ownership restrictions. In such condos, units are intended solely for the occupancy of the unit owner. While renting out one or more bedrooms within your unit to roommates is permissible, you must also reside in the unit yourself.

PROS:

- Ideal for long-term ownership, fostering a strong sense of pride among unit owners who tend to maintain their units and the overall condo community.

- Owners in these condos often maintain positive relationships with fellow unit owners.

- Renting out spare bedrooms is allowed, providing potential rental income.

- High owner occupancy rates can facilitate easier resale to another buyer, meeting FHA requirements.

The Smart Home Buyer

CONS:

- Units cannot be rented to tenants. If you plan to travel for an extended period or relocate short-term, this type of condo may not suit your needs.
- Not suitable for short-term ownership.
- Some unit owners may exhibit intense passion for their condos, which can be overwhelming for some buyers.
- Reduces the pool of potential buyers when selling, as some prefer the flexibility to rent out their units if necessary.

Warrantable vs. Non-Warrantable (Risky):

When it comes to obtaining a mortgage for a condominium, the distinction between warrantable and non-warrantable condos is crucial. Mortgages are typically backed by government-sponsored enterprises such as Freddie Mac or Fannie Mae, which set basic requirements for loans to receive backing for conventional mortgages. Condos that fail to meet these requirements are classified as non-warrantable, presenting challenges for potential buyers.

Lenders earn profits by issuing mortgages and selling them in the secondary market. However, secondary enterprises rarely purchase non-warrantable loans, causing banks to hesitate in holding such loans for extended periods. Consequently, non-warrantable loans typically come with higher costs, including increased down payment requirements and higher interest rates.

One common reason why a condo may not be warrantable is if it has less than 50% owner occupancy. Consequently, you may encounter condos that are 100% owner-occupied, or the condo association may impose limits on the number of units that can be rented out at any given time.

Marc Saint Clair, MBA

What to Consider During Condo Showings:

- Check for Smoke Odors: Investigate whether potential neighbors, especially those adjacent to or below your unit, are smokers. A discreet way to discern this is by smelling the inside of a closet, as some agents may attempt to mask odors. Recognizing nearby smokers is crucial, as it may influence your decision, given that many sellers seek to distance themselves from such environments.

- Talk to Neighbors: Engage in conversations with current neighbors to gather insights into the building's safety and security. Inquire about any known incidents of theft or police calls within the community. Their firsthand experiences can provide valuable information influencing your decision.

- FHA Approval: Verify if the condo has received approval for FHA financing, as it can affect your eligibility for certain loans. Being aware of the condo's FHA approval status helps you make informed decisions regarding financing options.

- Noise and Flooring: Ask about materials used to separate floors between units, as concrete flooring is preferable for noise absorption, especially with children. Inquire whether the floors are carpeted or hardwood, as this choice can affect noise levels within the condo.

- Condo Fees and Assessments: Request information about current condo fees and any ongoing or upcoming assessments. Understanding these financial obligations is vital for assessing your budget and financial commitments.

- Assessment History: Inquire about assessments from the past three years to gauge the true financial obligations associated with the condo. There are condos with forever assessments. They have low condo fees, but you can see after due diligence that they have assessments every year, thereby hiding the true cost of the condo fees.

The Smart Home Buyer

- Meeting Minutes and Financials: Review meeting minutes and financial reports from the latest condo association meeting to gain insights into the condo community's culture, financial stability, and any upcoming projects or decisions.

Smoking:

Most condos do not have a smoking ban in place, so beware. I once had a client who endured this unfortunate ordeal. Their downstairs neighbor epitomized the nightmare smoker. Smoke naturally ascends, infiltrating their living space through thin sheetrock, kitchen vents, heating baseboard holes, and even the hardwood floor. Stepping into their unit on an average day was like entering a smoky bar. The pungent odor permeated everything — clothing, bed sheets, and the entire household. The stench became an unwelcome companion, following them everywhere. They resorted to multiple air purifiers and kept their kitchen exhaust running around the clock, spending a small fortune on frequent filter replacements. Their electric bill soared, making them the neighborhood's highest spender. Financial woes were just the tip of the iceberg; they also grappled with deteriorating health. Asthma worsened, breathing became difficult, and hospital visits increased due to heightened smoke exposure.

Summer brought new challenges. They couldn't turn on their air conditioner because the neighbor downstairs kept their windows open. Any attempt to cool their home resulted in the AC unit inhaling fresh cigarette smoke from below, circulating it throughout their space. They had to strategize, running the AC only when the neighbors were away or late at night when the smokers were inactive, turning their lives into a constant balancing act. Their home became a place they tried to spend as little time in as possible, involuntarily inhaling their neighbors' cigarette smoke for hours each day.

The reality is that cigarette smoke contains over 4,000 chemicals, including 43 known carcinogens and 400 other toxins. According to the Surgeon General, there is no safe level of exposure to secondhand smoke. Even small amounts of exposure can be harmful, especially for children, who are more susceptible to lung problems, ear infections, and severe asthma due to this exposure. The 2010 U.S. Surgeon General's Report on How Tobacco Smoke Causes Disease underscores that even occasional exposure to secondhand smoke is detrimental. It can rapidly inflame and damage blood vessel linings, increasing the risk of heart attacks and strokes.

Owning a house with smoking neighbors not only takes a toll on your finances but also jeopardizes your health. Sadly, it is not a mandatory disclosure in many cases. Without thorough research, you might unknowingly purchase a property that conceals this hidden hazard, turning your dream home into an unexpected nightmare.

Chapter 11
Offer and Deal Structure

ANATOMY OF AN OFFER:

While the specific legal content of an offer can vary widely by state and region, it typically includes the following components: the offer amount, contingencies, mortgage pre-approval or bank statement, and the offer's earnest money deposit. Sometimes, the best offer is not necessarily the highest offer. Often times, it is what are some of the conditions you write in the offer.

SELLER PREFERENCE:

When it comes to seller preferences, their primary objective is to find a buyer who can deliver a seamless and timely closing. In the eyes of sellers, strength in a buyer is often demonstrated by certain practices. For instance, a strong buyer may opt for a cash offer, providing the seller with the assurance of a swift and uncomplicated transaction. Alternatively, they might present an offer backed by a preapproval for a conventional loan, signaling their financial stability and commitment to the purchase.

Typical Financing methodology order of preference for sellers:

1. Cash
2. Conventional Loan
3. FHA

Down Payment:

One hallmark of a strong buyer is their willingness to put down a substantial earnest money deposit, typically around 20% or more of the purchase price. This significant deposit not only underscores their sincerity but also provides the seller with a sense of security.

Contingencies:

Furthermore, strong buyers may choose to streamline the process by minimizing or waiving contingencies. While contingencies can protect the buyer's interests, they can also prolong the closing timeline and introduce uncertainty. A strong buyer, therefore, might opt to limit or forego contingencies altogether, instilling confidence in the seller about a smooth transaction.

It's worth noting that FHA loans, while a valuable financing option for many buyers are sometimes perceived as less desirable by sellers due to the stringent nature of these loans. I have encountered situations where sellers have chosen a lower conventional offer over a higher FHA offer.

NEGOTIATION STRATEGIES

We will look at some negotiation tactics that can help you secure a favorable deal. You will need to balance your risk versus opportunity adequately.

Escalation Clause:

An escalation clause is a strategy used by a buyer to increase their offer price automatically if competing offers are higher than their initial offer. It's, in essence, an insurance mechanism that will stretch your initial offer to your maximum would-be offer.

Here's how it works, along with its pros and cons:

Offer: The buyer submits their offer along with the purchase price they're willing to pay for the property.

Escalation Amount: Within the offer, the buyer includes an escalation clause that states how much they're willing to increase

The Smart Home Buyer

their offer in response to competing offers. For example, they might offer $500,000 with an escalation clause that increases their bid by $3,000 above any competing offer, up to a maximum of $550,000, provided that their preapproval goes to that amount.

Competing Offers: If another buyer submits another higher offer, the escalation clause automatically raises the buyer's offer to the predetermined amount above the highest competing offer. In this case, if the other offer was $510,000, the escalation clause automatically raises the buyer's offer to $513,000.

Pros of an Escalation Clause:

- Competitive Advantage**:** In a competitive market, it gives you an edge. Your offer would always be cataloged ahead to a point.
- Transparent: It demonstrates your motivation to get the property.
- Time-Saving: It eliminates back-and-forth with the seller.

Cons of an Escalation Clause:

- Seller Awareness: You show your card how far you are willing to go.
- Overpaying: You might end up paying more than you originally intended if competing offers are significantly higher.
- Seller's Advantage: Sellers can use your escalation clause to their advantage by disclosing fake competing offers or pushing your offer to its limit. To this you can also ask for proof of the highest offer.
- Complexity: It adds complexity to the offer and may require

careful drafting to avoid loopholes and disputes.

Appraisal Contingency:

Include a contingency in your offer subject to the property's appraisal. This ensures that if the property doesn't appraise for the agreed-upon purchase price, you will receive your money back. Some confident buyers choose to keep this contingency in place, as sellers often view it favorably. However, it's essential to have extra funds available in case the appraisal comes in lower than expected.

If the property doesn't appraise for the agreed price, most sellers are open to renegotiating. They may ask the buyer to cover part of the difference between the appraised value and the agreed price. As a buyer, it's important to be strategic in your response. While some sellers may suggest splitting the difference 50/50, you can choose to decline, offer a smaller contribution, or agree to split the difference.

It's worth noting that property appraisals typically hold steady for several months, though there are exceptions. In rare cases, an appraisal done within 30 days of another may come back higher due to recent comparable sales that affect the property's valuation. Therefore, use your judgment when negotiating any adjustments to the price. If the seller refuses to lower the price or compromise, they may decide not to proceed with the sale.

Appraisal adjustment:

Offering more than the market value, expecting an appraisal decrease.

Offering more than the market value of a property with the expectation of an appraisal decrease, leading the seller to lower the price, is a risky strategy. While some buyers may attempt this approach, it's important to recognize its low success rate and potential drawbacks. In some cases, the appraisal may indeed align

The Smart Home Buyer

with the inflated offer price, leaving the buyer obligated to proceed with the purchase at that higher price point. This outcome can result in financial strain and dissatisfaction for the buyer. Therefore, while this tactic has been employed, I strongly discourage it due to its inherent risks and limited effectiveness in achieving the desired outcome.

Time to Move Out:

Offer flexibility is a valuable negotiation strategy that involves adjusting certain aspects of your offer to better align with the seller's preferences, making your offer more appealing to them.

If the seller needs extra time to move out, perhaps because they are relocating out of state or awaiting completion of their new home, you can offer them the flexibility to stay in the house for a few additional days after closing. This Seller Lease-Back or Rent-Back arrangement can be made at the cost of a daily or weekly fee, typically equivalent to your daily mortgage payment. However, it's essential to consider the risks associated with having the seller remain in the property as a short-term tenant. Additionally, check with your lender, as most loans have a move-in date requirement by which you must take possession of the property.

Make Repairs:

Another way to make your offer more competitive is to address basic repairs such as painting the trim. Peeling paint on the exterior of the house can be a concern for FHA loans, as it may be flagged by the FHA appraiser. To preemptively address this issue, some FHA buyers offer to paint any peeling areas at their own expense before the FHA appraiser's visit. By offering this solution, buyers can make their offer more appealing and level the playing field with conventional loan offers.

Flexible closing date:

Flexibility with the closing date can also enhance your offer's appeal. Some buyers are willing to set closing dates beyond the typical timeframe to accommodate the seller's preferences. For example, buyers may extend the closing date by up to three months to provide the seller with peace of mind and allow them to sell on their own terms. However, it's crucial to be mindful of rate locks when extending the closing date. Once the bank locks your interest rate, typically after the Purchase and Sale Agreement is signed, you have a limited time to close. Extending the rate lock period may incur additional fees.

Paying for rate lock:

Paying for rate lock extensions can be a risky but effective strategy. In this scenario, the buyer indicates their willingness to wait for up to three months for the seller to find suitable housing and agrees to cover the cost of extending the rate lock. Working with a reliable mortgage broker can help minimize expenses, as they can monitor the rate changes and lock in the rate when the seller secures suitable housing.

Exclusion list:

Buyers may also consider forgoing appliances listed in the exclusion list. Some sellers include an exclusion list of items they prefer not to include in the sale, such as appliances. However, buyers who are interested in these appliances may offer a higher purchase price to include them. Excluding items from the exclusion list can be a strategic move, as these items may hold sentimental value for the seller, making them more open to negotiation on other terms of the offer.

Heating Fuel & Propane Tanks:

The Smart Home Buyer

There is an annoying practice where, at closing, the seller would present the buyer with an invoice for reimbursement for the amount of fuel present on premise at the time of closing. Make sure to include that in your offer as one of the contingencies along with appliances.

Solar Panels:

When purchasing a home with solar panels, buyers should be aware of the different ownership arrangements. Some solar panels are owned outright, which is advantageous for buyers. However, others may be leased, and the lease is transferred with the sale of the property. It's essential for buyers with credit scores under 700, especially those in the mid-600s, to exercise caution, as solar companies may require a credit check for the transfer. This credit inquiry could potentially lower the buyer's credit score, posing a risk to their loan eligibility.

There are two examples I want to share with you. In the first case, a client had a credit score of around 640 needed to maintain a minimum credit score of 620 for their loan package. To avoid jeopardizing their eligibility, they chose to ignore all communication with the solar panel company until after closing. It worked.

In another situation, the lender wanted a transfer approval letter from the solar company before issuing an approval letter for closing. The buyer had no option but to complete the solar lease application and credit check. The buyer expressed concerns with her lender that the credit check might affect the loan. The lender assured the buyer that they would not check her credit before closing, given that the credit check they had on file would not expire. This approach also worked for her. Every situation is different.

Additionally, leased solar panels function similarly to other leases, impacting the buyer's debt-to-income ratio. The solar lease is usually transferred after the closing. Therefore, buyers on the cusp of their purchasing capacity should approach solar panels with caution.

Marc Saint Clair, MBA

Mutually Agreed Upon P&S:

Ensure that your offer is contingent upon reaching a mutually agreed-upon purchase and sales agreement. This safeguard becomes crucial in case disagreements arise during the negotiation stage, providing an added layer of protection for your deposit.

Financing:

When making an offer on a property, it's prudent to include a contingency clause subject to financing. Life can bring unexpected changes, and ensuring your deposit is protected is paramount. By including this contingency, you safeguard your deposit; if you're unable to secure the necessary loan for purchasing the property, you'll receive your money back. This clause provides reassurance and financial protection in case your financing falls through, allowing you to proceed with confidence in your home-buying journey.

Broom Swept Condition and clear of debris:

To guarantee the property is handed over to you in a clean and debris-free condition, include a provision stating, "Subject to property being delivered in broom swept condition and free of yard, garage and attic debris." This ensures any unwanted items are removed before your possession.

Cash Back for Closing:

If you require cash back to cover closing costs, specify in your offer that it is subject to receiving a predetermined amount ($x.xx) for closing costs and pre-paid items. Ensure your agent includes "subject to $$ back for closing and pre-paid items" to encompass any expenses not directly related to closing costs. Any unused funds will revert to the seller, so your agent and mortgage broker should strategize to exhaust the allocated amount creatively. In case of surplus funds, consider purchasing points to lower your interest rate effectively.

TIPS:

Offering significantly below the asking price, especially by more than 10%, may indeed lead to your offer being disregarded by some sellers. However, it's essential to consider factors such as market conditions, property specifics, and the seller's motivation.

Step Four
My Offer is Accepted, Now What?

Chapter 12
Inspection

Congratulations on having your offer accepted! Now that you've secured your place, it's time to focus on completing your Purchase and Sales Agreement, typically within 7-10 days. This comprehensive document outlines the terms, conditions, and obligations of both you and the seller.

If your offer included a home inspection contingency, it's crucial to proceed with scheduling a home inspection promptly. Even if you didn't include this contingency, I strongly recommend arranging for a home inspection before closing, if the seller allows or any time after closing. Addressing issues upfront can save you headaches down the road.

For those with a home inspection contingency, prior research should have identified two to three reliable home inspectors. Given their busy schedules, especially during peak seasons like spring, having multiple options ensures you can secure an inspection appointment promptly.

Home inspectors are trained to identify various issues with the property, from minor concerns to major structural issues or environmental hazards like mold.

Following the inspection, you'll have several options:
- Walk away, if the findings are overwhelming.
- Negotiate repairs or financial adjustments with the seller.
- Proceed with the purchase as-is.

When requesting repairs, sellers are typically more inclined to address safety-related issues, such as exposed wires or well water concerns. Alternatively, you can negotiate a price reduction to cover the cost of repairs. For example, if fixing the central air conditioning system would cost $1,000, you could ask the seller to reduce the price or provide a credit toward closing costs.

In cases where repairs cannot be completed before closing, sellers may opt to prepay for the repairs or provide funds to cover the costs post-closing.

Additionally, certain inspections may be necessary depending on the property's features:

Well Water:

Testing the quality of well water is highly advisable during the home inspection process, especially if it is the primary source of drinking water. Many of my buyers have discovered unacceptable levels of contaminants in their water samples. Common issues include nitrates, coliform bacteria, and pH levels, among others. In each case, we have required the sellers to cover the costs of mitigation efforts, such as installing filters and water treatment systems, which often run into the thousands of dollars. I also recommend periodic testing even after purchase to ensure ongoing water quality.

Termite & Pest:

If termite activity is suspected, a termite expert can further investigate, and remediation may be required.

Radon:

In regions prone to radon exposure, testing for this naturally occurring gas is recommended, with mitigation systems available if needed.

Marc Saint Clair, MBA

Asbestos:

Asbestos is commonly found in homes built before the mid-1980s, necessitating careful evaluation and possibly negotiations with the seller if detected. Asbestos may be present in various materials such as insulation, siding, floor tiles, pipe insulation, and more.

Vents:

Improperly placed vents, such as those ending in the attic, may need correction to ensure proper ventilation.

Your home inspector will assist in identifying these issues, and your real estate agent will guide you through negotiating with the seller if that is an option. Whether it's requesting repairs, price reductions, or cash back credit at closing to cover repair cost, there are various approaches to address post-inspection findings and ensure a smooth transaction. If you decide to walk away from a deal following an inspection, your contract should include an inspection contingency that allows you to do so without penalty, safeguarding your earnest money deposit.

Chapter 13
Purchase and Sales Agreement

Once your offer has been accepted and the home inspection completed, the next crucial step in the home-buying process is the Purchase and Sales Agreement (P&S Agreement). Ideally, you should begin searching for an attorney either before or immediately after your offer is accepted. Your agent or attorney will then facilitate communication with the seller regarding any desired changes to the original offer based on the findings of the home inspection.

The P&S Agreement stands as one of the most critical documents in the sales process. It contains essential details such as parties involved, timelines, due diligence obligations, and responsibilities of both buyer and seller until after closing. Additionally, it addresses contingencies such as property damage before closing and outlines procedures for handling deposits in case of conflicts.

Once the parties reach a mutual resolution on any inspection findings, the seller's attorney will send a draft copy of the P&S Agreement to the buyer's attorney. The buyer's attorney will then review and revise the draft as needed before sending it back to the seller's attorney for approval. This negotiation process may involve multiple rounds until a final draft acceptable to both parties is achieved.

Attorneys often include addendums to further clarify specific clauses within the P&S Agreement. Additionally, if any changes are required, such as adding a spouse's name or extending timelines, an amendment to the P&S Agreement is warranted.

After thorough review and negotiation, both buyer and seller must sign the finalized P&S Agreement. At this stage, the buyer typically provides a second check to bind the agreement. While sellers may prefer the entire down payment at this point, strategically, buyers should aim to provide as little as possible. This approach safeguards against potential issues and ensures minimal financial risk in case the deal falls through. Therefore, it's advisable to negotiate to minimize the initial financial commitment when binding the Purchase and Sales Agreement.

The Smart Home Buyer

Step Five
Close

Marc Saint Clair, MBA

Chapter 14
After Purchase and Sale & Before Closing

With the Purchase and Sales Agreement signed, the focus shifts to the period between agreement and closing, where numerous behind-the-scenes activities unfold. During this time, your lender initiates their due diligence to secure your loan, engaging an attorney to represent the bank's interests. It's essential to understand that the bank attorney's role is to ensure all requirements are met on behalf of the bank, and their fees are typically included in your closing costs.

Over the next three weeks, although outwardly quiet, several crucial tasks are underway:

Insurance Binder:

Your first task is obtaining an insurance binder, which provides a quote and coverage description for the first year. You can opt to pay for this upfront or at closing. Shopping around for quotes from multiple insurance companies is advisable, as various discounts may be available. It's worth inquiring about potential discounts you may qualify for, such as bundling home and auto insurance.

Appraisal:

You'll need to prepay for the appraisal, which is conducted once payment is made to the mortgage company. An appraiser will assess the property's value, with the resulting report shared with both the mortgage broker and yourself.

Title Search:

The closing attorney conducts a title search to ensure you receive a clear title, free of any liens, encumbrances, or ownership issues. This step is crucial in securing your ownership rights to the property.

The Smart Home Buyer

Underwriting:

During this stage, the lender meticulously verifies your income, assets, debts, and other pertinent factors related to obtaining the loan. The goal is to assess the property's worth, your ability to repay the loan, and the likelihood of repayment. The underwriter may contact your employer and scrutinize all submitted documents. Depending on various factors, your loan may be approved, denied, or approved with conditions. The lender usually pulls your credit one last time to see if your credit condition is the same as when you walked through their front door. If issues arise, such as a high debt-to-income ratio, the underwriter may request actions like paying off certain debts to meet requirements. This is where working with an experienced mortgage broker is worth its weight in gold. I have been through many closings where the inexperienced mortgage broker was not able to identify simple or complex issues with the buyer due to their lack of experience. Buyers are subsequently marched into closing only to be denied at the underwriting stage well after significant time, emotional, and financial investments on the part of the buyer. It is important to select an experienced mortgage broker who can anticipate challenges and guide you through the process, minimizing surprises during underwriting.

Commitment Letter:

If your loan is approved, you'll receive a commitment letter or conditional commitment letter outlining the documentation requirements for finalizing the loan. This letter serves as a confirmation of the loan approval, detailing any outstanding conditions that need to be met for the loan to proceed to closing.

Navigating these steps with careful attention to detail and the guidance of experienced professionals helps ensure a smooth transition from purchase agreement to closing.

Chapter 15
The Closing

Congratulations! You've reached the final stretch of your home-buying journey. After receiving the commitment letter, all parties agree on a closing date, and you may also schedule a final walk-through with the seller. This inspection allows you to ensure that the property is in the agreed-upon condition before signing the final paperwork. It's advisable to schedule the final walk-through within 24 hours of closing to address any last-minute concerns.

Closing Costs:

Your closing costs encompass various charges, which can vary depending on your location, loan type, and lender. Here are some common expenses you might encounter:

- Heating Fuel Cost: If not included in the offer, the seller may invoice you at closing for heating fuel remaining in the tank.
- Tax Adjustment: Reimbursement to the seller for prepaid taxes if the quarter is not yet over.
- Property Tax: Escrow for three months of property taxes, with adjustments made after closing as needed.
- Lender Origination Charge: Fee from your lender for loan processing.
- Appraisal Fee: Cost of property appraisal if not prepaid.
- Credit Report Fee: Expense for credit report checks.
- Upfront Mortgage Insurance Premium (MIP): Insurance fee for FHA loans.
- Flood Certificate: Certification of flood zone status.
- Prepaid Interest: Daily interest cost from closing to the start

The Smart Home Buyer

of the first mortgage payment.

- Homeowners Insurance: Premium if not prepaid.
- Title Settlement, Exam, Prep Fee: Charge from the closing attorney's office for title-related services.
- Owner's Title Insurance: One-time fee to protect the buyer from title defects.
- Lender's Title Insurance: One-time fee to protect the lender.
- Government Recording and Transfer Charges: Fees for recording documents and municipal lien certificates.
- Plot Plan, Survey Fee: Survey costs to verify property boundaries and compliance with zoning regulations.
- Homestead: Provides property tax relief and legal shield from unsecured debt to homeowners who use their property as their primary residence.
- Closing Attorney Fees: Charges from the closing attorney's office.
- Buyer Attorney Fees: If applicable, fees for buyer's attorney representation.
- Identification: Bring a valid government-issued photo ID, Social Security number, proof of residence, and any additional documentation requested by the lender or title company.

If you are not a US citizen, can you buy a house?

YES, absolutely; it's crucial to communicate openly with your lender about your immigration status and inquire whether they offer financing options tailored to your situation. Different lenders may have varying policies regarding the types of immigration statuses they accept for mortgage loans. By discussing your specific circumstances with your lender upfront, you can gain clarity on whether you're eligible for financing and explore any available options that align with your needs and goals.

Payment and Final Steps:

Before closing, the closing attorney will provide a final amount due, combining closing costs with part of the down payment. This payment is typically required in the form of a bank check or wire transfer. Additionally, ensure you bring valid, unexpired picture identification to verify your identity.

As you approach the closing, keep in mind the importance of understanding and preparing for these costs and requirements. With thorough preparation and guidance from your real estate team, you'll soon complete your home purchase and embark on the exciting journey of homeownership.

Signing the Documents:

At the closing, you'll meet with the closing attorney to sign the final paperwork. This includes the mortgage documents, title transfer documents, and any other legal agreements related to the transaction. Take your time to review each document carefully, and don't hesitate to ask questions if anything is unclear. If your schedule does not permit you to attend the closing, you can ask the closing attorney to let you sign your closing documents the night before.

Funding and Title Transfer:

Once all parties have signed the necessary documents, the closing attorney awaits the arrival of the lender's funds by wire transfer to fully fund the transaction. Once all funds are received and fully funded, the title transfer process officially commences.

The closing attorney then proceeds to record the necessary documents with the registry of deeds. This is commonly termed "on record." Upon recording, the title transfer becomes official, and ownership of the property legally transfers from the seller to the buyer. This step is crucial in ensuring that the transaction is properly documented and legally recognized by the relevant authorities.

Receiving the Keys:

After the closing is complete, all parties eagerly await confirmation from the closing attorney that the necessary documents have been recorded. Once the attorney confirms that the transaction is officially recorded, the keys to the property are transferred to you, the buyer.

The physical transfer of keys can occur in various ways. Some sellers may leave the keys with the closing attorney to be picked up by the buyer after recording. Alternatively, the keys may be transferred from the seller's side to your buyer agent, who holds them until confirmation of recording. Sellers or their agents may use lockboxes, leave the keys under a mat, or personally hand them over to your agent. The method of transfer can vary widely and is often determined by the preferences of the parties involved.

Post-Closing Tasks:

Following the closing, there are several important tasks to complete to ensure a smooth transition into your new home. One of the first priorities is to change the locks for enhanced security. Consider bringing a drill and a set of new locks to facilitate this process shortly after closing. Additionally, there are several administrative tasks to address, including setting up utilities in your name, updating your address with relevant parties, and coordinating any necessary repairs or renovations before moving in.

To streamline the transition process, it's helpful for your agent to obtain the following information from the seller before closing, if applicable:

Marc Saint Clair, MBA

1. Name of the electric company.
2. Name of the gas company.
3. Name of the oil/propane company (if applicable).
4. List and copies of all warranties for appliances or home systems.
5. Schedule for trash/recycle pickup in the neighborhood.
6. Any neighborhood traditions or community events to be aware of.
7. Information about solar panels, including warranties or maintenance requirements.
8. Home Owner's Association (HOA) information if you haven't done so.
9. Key contacts of repairman, HVAC companies, electricians that did previous work that know the property.
10. Home security system info, if any.
11. Mail and package delivery instructions. An important consideration is handling deliveries during wintertime. In some towns, mail carriers are not required to deliver mail if homeowners have not cleared snow from their paths. It's essential to ensure walkways and access points are shoveled to avoid disruptions in mail and package delivery.
12. Other recommendations or unknowns about the property.

Celebrating Your New Home:

Finally, take a moment to celebrate this significant milestone in your life. Whether it's with a small gathering of friends and family or a quiet moment of reflection, acknowledging your accomplishment and the excitement of starting this new chapter in your new home is

The Smart Home Buyer

essential.

In conclusion, embarking on the journey to homeownership requires careful planning, diligence, and the support of knowledgeable professionals. From the initial stages of house hunting to navigating the complexities of financing, negotiations, and closing, the process can be both exhilarating and challenging. However, armed with the right information and guidance, prospective buyers can confidently navigate each step, making informed decisions that align with their goals and priorities. By leveraging the insights shared in this comprehensive guide for smart home buyers, individuals can approach the home-buying process with confidence, knowing they have the tools and resources needed to make one of life's most significant investments.

Congratulations once again on your new home, and may it bring you years of joy and happiness!

Marc Saint Clair, MBA

Step Six
Bonus

Chapter 16
Buying Without a Buyer Agent: A New Era

The recent settlement reached by the National Association of Realtors (NAR) regarding real estate commissions will usher in significant changes concerning buyer representation by buyer agents. Although the settlement awaits court approval, its implications are far-reaching. It addresses the practice of charging both the seller and buyer agent fees, deeming it antitrust and driving commissions higher than justified by services rendered. This settlement aims to resolve pending lawsuits and encompasses over one million members of NAR, affiliated multiple listing services, and certain state and local realtor associations.

Traditionally, when a seller's agent lists a property, they negotiate a representation fee covering both the seller and buyer agent commissions. While contracts stipulate fee splitting, the actual division is often undisclosed and typically not evenly split, contrary to public assumption. More commonly, seller agents retain the larger share (4-3%), with buyer agents frequently given a 2% commission. This pattern persists despite variations in commission structures across markets and the ability of sellers to negotiate fees.

The Pros:

1. Sellers stand to benefit from reduced fees, retaining more proceeds at closing without paying for buyer agent services.

2. Increased competition among seller agents may lead to lower listing fees, offering sellers more options.

3. Prices of properties may decrease as buyers incur additional expenses at closing, potentially exerting downward pressure on home prices.

Marc Saint Clair, MBA

The Cons:

1. Buyers will bear additional fees for the representation of a buyer agent.
2. Those opting for buyer representation may face higher costs, as the buyer agent fee translates to cashback for closing.
3. Low-income, minority, and immigrant homebuyers will be disproportionately affected, potentially leading to decreased homeownership rates in these communities.
4. The absence of buyer agents may lead to discrimination, with sellers gaining access to buyer information that could influence their decisions.
5. Anticipated increases in housing discrimination cases against homeowners and seller agents could further exacerbate disparities.

Protecting Yourself When Hiring a Buyer Agent: How to Avoid Excessive Fees:

When engaging a buyer agent, they will typically present a contract that stipulates their compensation, which usually ranges between 2-4% of the purchase price, payable at closing. The contract may also include a clause stating that if the agent cannot secure their commission from the seller, the buyer is obligated to pay the difference. For example, on a $500,000 home, a 1% commission equals $5,000, which can significantly impact the buyer's financial planning.

To avoid being caught off-guard, I advise all buyers to request an addendum to the buyer agent agreement. This addendum should include language similar to the following: (An addendum is an extra document added to a contract to modify or add terms. It's written separately and becomes part of the contract once signed by all parties. It's used when both sides agree to adjust or add something to the original agreement.)

The Smart Home Buyer

"In the event the seller does not pay the full or partial commission, we will renegotiate the contract, capping the buyer's obligation to a flat fee of $4,000 (or another mutually agreed-upon amount). If the seller contributes at least this minimum amount, the buyer's obligation is considered fulfilled. If the seller contributes less than this amount or nothing at all, the buyer's responsibility remains capped at $4,000. Any surplus fees provided by the seller will be retained by the buyer agent."

By negotiating this type of agreement upfront, you can safeguard against unexpected financial burdens and ensure that your interests are protected throughout the transaction. It's always wise to have a real estate attorney review any agreements before signing, to ensure clarity and fairness in your obligations.

The lawsuit's implications threaten to undermine decades of efforts to promote fair housing. Government intervention is imperative to prevent potential abuse. Outside of that, a technological solution enabling blind offers without disclosing personal information might be the way to go. For this reason, I have personally embarked on a journey to create an AI platform that will help home buyers place offers without disclosing personal information.

Tips for Buying in the New Era:

1. Utilize electronic platforms to remotely submit offers, including information from your mortgage broker and directing financing inquiries to them.
2. Negotiate a flat-rate agreement with a buyer agent to offer drafting assistance, foregoing open house visits.
3. Make offers contingent upon satisfactory home inspections to mitigate risks in the absence of buyer agent guidance.

Marc Saint Clair, MBA

TIPS: How to deal with Housing Discrimination

If you are a buyer who didn't use a buyer agent, feel they've been discriminated against during the offer or purchase of a home due to their race, creed, religion, sexual orientation, or other protected characteristics, feel that their offers were not accepted due to discrimination you should act quickly by taking the following steps:

Home buyers in the United States have several avenues to file complaints or reports:

1. **U.S. Department of Housing and Urban Development (HUD):**

    HUD enforces the Fair Housing Act, which prohibits discrimination in housing based on race, color, national origin, religion, sex, familial status, or disability.

    Complaints can be filed online through the:

    HUD website:
    https://www.hud.gov/program_offices/fair_housing_equal_opp/online-complaint

    Phone: 1-800-669-9777

    Mail:
    https://www.hud.gov/program_offices/fair_housing_equal_opp/contact_fheo

    Visit HUD's Fair Housing Complaint Process for more information.

2. **State Fair Housing Agencies:**

    Many states have their own agencies that enforce state laws against housing discrimination, which may include additional protections beyond those covered by federal law.

    Buyers can file a complaint with their state's fair housing agency. Contact information can usually be found on the state government's website.

This is a list here:

https://www.hud.gov/program_offices/fair_housing_equal_opp/partners/FHAP/agencies

3. **Local Fair Housing Organizations:**

Local non-profit organizations dedicated to fair housing also assist individuals who believe they have been victims of housing discrimination. They may offer legal advice, advocacy, and assistance in filing complaints.

The National Fair Housing Alliance (NFHA) offers resources and can help find local organizations.

4. **State Attorney General's Office:**

The attorney general's office in each state can provide information on how to file a complaint if you've been subject to discrimination. Some states have a specific Civil Rights Division that handles such cases.

https://en.wikipedia.org/wiki/State_attorney_general

5. **The Equal Rights Center or American Civil Liberties Union (ACLU):**

These and similar organizations may offer additional resources or legal assistance for cases of discrimination. https://www.aclu.org

When filing a complaint, it's important to gather and present any evidence of discrimination, such as emails, texts, documents, or witness statements, to support the claim. Acting promptly is also crucial, as there are time limits for filing complaints under various laws.

Marc Saint Clair, MBA

Chapter 17
Home Owership by Non-Citizens

This chapter addresses a common question posed by my clients regarding the feasibility of purchasing property in the United States as a non-citizen. Hopefully, it addresses the various situations that I was presented with. The United States is an open market. If you are not a US citizen nor a permanent resident, you can legally purchase property in the US. If you are an undocumented resident, non-resident, refugee, asylum seeker, DACA recipient, or anyone living outside of the US, you can also purchase property in the US. There are currently no regulations or laws that prevent foreigners from owning property in the US. Regardless of your immigration status, you are protected under fair housing laws. If you have to leave the country due to deportation or any other circumstance, you do not lose ownership of the property. You can hire a management company to manage it in your absence.

Financing the Purchase

Now that we've cleared the legal aspect of owning a home, the next issue is how a non-citizen can finance a purchase. Depending on the classification of the non-citizen, there are certain options available. For every situation below, the steps are as follows:

1. Do a search for the suggested lender online. Identity 2-4 lenders.
2. Reach out to one or more and explain your situation.
3. Apply for a loan.
4. Get a pre-approval letter.
5. Hire an agent and search for a home.

The Smart Home Buyer

Permanent Residents

If you are a green card holder, you are a permanent resident. As such, you would qualify for all types of loan products as if you were a US citizen. All you would need are the basics: credit, income history, and down payment requirements, among others.

Loans you might be qualified for:

FHA, conventional, VA, USDA, Freddy Mac Choice, Fannie Mae Homestyle.

Documentation requirements include:

Green card, social security number, and driver's license.

Visas holders

Visa Holders If you are a non-permanent resident with an E1, E2, H1B, H2A, H2B, H3, G1, G2, G3, G4, or L1 Visa, you will be able to get a regular government-backed loan from most lenders as long as you can provide proof of current work history, down payment, credit history, along with two years' worth of income and tax return history.

Loans you might be qualified for:

FHA, conventional, VA, USDA, Freddy Mac Choice, Fannie Mae Homestyle.

Documentation requirements include:

Identification such as a passport, social security number, or ITIN number, and lastly, an official document from US Citizenship and Immigration Services (USCIS) confirming your residency right.

Marc Saint Clair, MBA

Refugee and Asylum Seekers with Legal Status

If you are an asylum seeker or refugee with an employment authorization form pending on the lender, you might be able to get a government-backed mortgage similar to someone with a green card. You must provide proof of current work history, down payment, and credit history, along with two years' worth of income and tax return history.

Loans you might be qualified for:

FHA, conventional, VA, USDA, Freddy Mac Choice, Fannie Mae Homestyle.

Documentation requirements include:

Employment authorization document, identification such as a foreign passport, and an official document from US Citizenship and Immigration Services (USCIS) that confirms your residency right.

DACA

If you are a child who was brought to the United States without documentation (DREAMER), you might be able to get an FHA loan or other loans similar to someone with a green card. You must provide proof of current work history, down payment, and credit history, along with two years' worth of income and tax return history.

Loans you might be qualified for:

FHA, conventional, VA, USDA, Freddy Mac Choice, Fannie Mae Homestyle.

Documentation requirements include:

Social security number or ITIN, driver's license, and employment authorization document.

Undocumented Living in the US

If you live in the US and have no social security card or no other legal status, cash purchase is the easiest and least challenging methodology for financing a purchase. It is possible to finance the purchase with a mortgage. While it will require determination and persistence, it can be done.

Loans you might be qualified for:

ITIN loan or Foreign National Loan.

To obtain an ITIN loan, you must apply for an ITIN number. The last section of this chapter is dedicated to how to successfully obtain an ITIN number.

You can obtain a Foreign National Loan with no social security number, no green card, and no visa. Creditworthiness, income stability, and ability to repay the loan are important factors that lenders assess when making a loan. If you are able to demonstrate creditworthiness through alternative means or from the credit system of your country of origin, you might be able to bypass the need for a US FICO credit score. Some lenders provide loans for non-residents living in the US, and others for non-residents living outside of the US. The requirements vary widely from one lender to the next, but in general, these are some of the requirements.

Documentation requirements:

US driver's license, Visa, or foreign passport.

Social Security or an Individual Taxpayer Identification Number (ITIN).

Proof of asset (Bank statement, Income).

Tax returns from native country if US tax return not available.

Other documentation that the lender might require.

Living outside of the US

If you live outside the US, you can buy property in the US. Aside from buying it outright with cash, you can finance the purchase through a couple of different mortgage programs.

Loans you might be qualified for:

Foreign National Loan or Foreign National DSCR Loan.

They will require a high down payment amount from approximately 20% to as much as 50%.

The DSCR loan would be based on the cash flow of the property you are planning on buying.

Documentation requirements:

Visa or foreign passport

Individual Taxpayer Identification Number (ITIN)

Proof of asset (Bank statement, Income).

Tax Returns from native country.

Other documentation that the lender might require.

Legal Considerations:

FIRPTA Regulations: The Foreign Investment in Real Property Tax Act (FIRPTA) imposes taxes on the sale or rental income of U.S. real estate by foreign nationals. Rental property income must be reported to the IRS, and taxes paid. When selling a property, non-U.S. citizens must comply with FIRPTA regulations, which may involve withholding a portion of the sale proceeds for tax purposes.

Financial Considerations:
1. Mortgage Options: Non-U.S. citizens may be eligible for various mortgage programs offered by U.S. lenders. These programs may have different eligibility criteria and down payment requirements. Exploring mortgage options tailored to non-U.S. citizens can help facilitate the home-buying process.
2. Down Payment: Lenders typically require a higher down payment from non-U.S. citizens compared to U.S. citizens. Saving a substantial amount for the down payment is crucial for securing financing and obtaining favorable loan terms.
3. Credit History: Establishing a solid credit history in the United States is essential for non-U.S. citizens seeking mortgage approval. Building credit through responsible financial behavior, such as timely bill payments and maintaining low credit card balances, can improve eligibility for mortgage loans.

Navigating the complexities of homeownership as a non-U.S. citizen requires careful planning, diligence, and expert guidance. By understanding the legal and financial considerations involved and leveraging available resources, non-U.S. citizens can achieve their dream of owning a home in the United States.

Marc Saint Clair, MBA

How to obtain an Individual Taxpayer Identification Number (ITIN)

- Step 1:
    - Visit the IRS Website: https://www.irs.gov/individuals/how-do-i-apply-for-an-itin
- Step 2:
    - Complete form W-7: https://www.irs.gov/pub/irs-pdf/fw7.pdf
    - Provide home country documentation including income, passport, school record, etc.
    - The more documentation, the better. Send W-7 to IRS along with documentation.
- Step 3:
    - Receive an ITIN number within 7 weeks.

Conclusion

In concluding this book, my deepest wish is for every individual, irrespective of their sex, religion, creed, or immigration status, to have the opportunity to experience the freedom and security of owning a home. Home ownership should not be restricted by arbitrary boundaries but should be a universal aspiration within reach for all who seek it. By understanding the legal frameworks, financial options, and pathways outlined in this book, I hope that more people can navigate and achieve their dreams of home ownership, contributing to vibrant and inclusive communities everywhere.

Made in the USA
Columbia, SC
27 September 2024